JOHN CHRYSOSTOM

JOHN
CHRYSOSTOM

Earl M. Blackburn

PUBLISHING WITH A MISSION

EP BOOKS
Faverdale North,
Darlington, DL3 0PH, England

e-mail: sales@epbooks.org
web: http://www.epbooks.org

133 North Hanover Street,
Carlisle, PA 17013, USA

e-mail: usasales@epbooks.org
web: http://www.epbooks.us

First published 2012

British Library Cataloguing in Publication Data available

ISBN-13   978-0-85234-772-0   ISBN-10: 0-85234-772-3

Printed and bound in Great Britain by Martin's the Printers Ltd, Berwick-upon-Tweed.

CONTENTS

PREFACE

I was taught that the preface should be written last. If true, then the last shall be first with regard to some esteemed people, who are owed very special thanks. Jim and Juliana Lipe graciously provided a beautiful and quiet place 'out in the country' where I could write without interruption. Courtney Kreid, my editorial assistant, and Billy Sutton gave helpful suggestions that offset my writing foibles. Two colleagues, whose friendship and fellowship in the gospel ministry has been prized for decades, Danald Lindblad and Tom Lyon, read my manuscript and made valuable suggestions. Several years ago, Pastor Lyon also gave me the thirty-nine volume set of the *Nicene and Post-Nicene Fathers*, which has proven its weight in gold for research. Arden Hodgins, a dear friend and a gifted servant of the Word, wrote a kind commendation. Dr Tom Nettles, a dear friend (in spite of his 'visceral reactions' against my split infinitives) and a church historian *par excellance*, did the same. Heritage Baptist Church in Shreveport, a delightful and generous church to pastor, lovingly gave me writing sabbaticals. My darling wife, Debby, the second greatest love of my life, behind Christ and his Word, has given me her unfailing love and service. What can I say to thank you? Words utterly fail me. Finally, to all the faithful servants of the Word around this globe, who consistently and boldly expound the whole counsel of God, your courage stirs me. What would the world be without you? May Christ give his churches a host of these Chrysostom-like preachers.

Earl M. Blackburn
Bossier City, Louisiana

INTRODUCTION

Golden Mouth — what a seemingly ostentatious name to identify one of the Greek Fathers of the early church! He had no part in shaping the historical Trinitarian or Christological controversies of his day. He played no role in the preceding, time-honoured ecumenical Church Councils of Nicaea and Constantinople before his installation as bishop. His forced bishopric of Constantinople lasted just under six years (398–404) and his tenure was fraught with political intrigue, petty envying, and intense strife. He had neither desire for politics nor ambition for ecclesiastical advancement. He preferred to live the simple life of an ascetic and had no cravings for the fame, riches, or luxuries that came with life in the metropolitan cities of his day. Twice he was deposed and banished contrary to canonical law. Betrayed, sick and exhausted, he died in exile, far away from home in present-day Georgia in 407.

Why, then, is he recognized by both the Eastern and Western branches of Christianity as one of the Doctors of the Church, but especially regarded as such by the East, rivalling only the Cappadocian Fathers (Basil the Great, Gregory of Nyssa, and Gregory of Nazianzus)? What has made him so revered and remembered? Why is it that today he is known in two of the three major branches of Christianity, as 'Saint' Chrysostom of Byzantium? What was it that caused the great Protestant Reformer of Geneva, John Calvin, to esteem him so highly as to publish a book of his particularly selected sermons? Why is it that every book on church history devotes a portion of its study of the early church to John Chrysostom? These are interesting questions indeed.

Golden Mouth was neither the birth name nor the ecclesiastical name given during John's life or ministry. He was simply named John and, no doubt, would have preferred it to remain that way. However, because of his golden eloquence in the pulpit, empowered by a mighty Spirit-anointed unction in his preaching of the Word of God, his renown enthusiastically lived on. Thus, sixth-century churchmen began regularly referring to him as 'Chrysostomos' which is Greek for 'golden mouthed'. (Chrysostom is the anglicized form of the Greek.) This name has been appended to John of Antioch ever since. Throughout history, the names of John and Chrysostom have been used interchangeably to refer to one and the same person, with Chrysostom being the more famous. However, throughout this book, the name of John will ordinarily be used, except when the context suits the use of Chrysostom.

TIMELINE

1

THE TIMES OF THE MAN

Many adversaries

Since the days of the Apostles, Christianity had grown, though not without intense struggles. Paul knew the reality of 'many adversaries' in his apostolic ministry (1 Corinthians 16:9), and earnest followers of Christ would know the same. Several enemies warred against Christianity on various fronts. The older pagan mythologies of Greece and Rome covered the world during the time of Paul and John. Shrines to various gods and goddesses were everywhere (e.g., Zeus/Jupiter, Poseidon/Neptune, Aphrodite/Venus). Then, Greece's demise and Rome's overwhelming rise led to the belief that the emperor was connected to the gods or even one of the gods incarnated, which led to the imperial cult of Caesar worship. Plus, there were older forms of the mystical cults (e.g., Isis in Egypt, Cybele in Asia Minor, Mithras in Persia), which normally involved ecstatic dancing, trances and sexual orgies. And, finally, there remained a blinded, raging Judaism, which had crucified the Messiah. Each spread throughout the empire and competed for the people's worship.

When they could not persuade adherents to turn away, these adversaries persecuted and sought to destroy the teachings and disciples of the humble Carpenter from Galilee. None succeeded. Using legal channels, authorities fined, imprisoned, confiscated the property of, tortured, dismembered, burned and killed many believers, who became known as martyrs. However, the more Christians they killed, the more rampantly Christianity grew. It was Tertullian (*c.* 160–225) who would later remind the persecuting world that 'You may kill us, but you will not destroy us. The blood of the martyrs is the seed of the church' (*Apologeticum*, 50). The large, but unstable, Roman Empire served as the internet through which the harried Christian message spread. And, spread it did! It is known from artefacts found in Yorkshire that the gospel had reached as far as Britain by the late first century.

Diocletian (244–331) became emperor in 284 and set about to stabilize and restructure the empire. He did this by declaring himself to be the supreme Augustus (emperor) and dividing the empire in two. Taking for himself the Eastern Empire in 286, Diocletian created a co-Augustus to rule the Western Empire. Then, in 292, he further divided each half (East and West) in two, creating a Caesar to rule each quarter under the authority of the two Augusti. There were four mini-empires in one. Contrary to what might be thought, these administrative manoeuvers made a strong organization that consolidated and somewhat extended the empire. It must be noted that while Latin was the primary language of the West, Greek was the dominant language in the East. Until Tertullian, the first theologian to write in Latin, all Christian theological literature was written in Greek.

World-changing events

Three major, interconnected events catapulted Christianity into a popular limelight. The first event was Constantine's victory to become the supreme ruler of the empire. After Diocletian's death, a fierce civil war ensued over who would become the sole Augustus. The two surviving contenders in the West, Constantine and Maxentius, both of whom were Caesars, came together in battle outside of Rome at Milvian Bridge, an important route over the Tiber River. Before the battle, Constantine allegedly had a vision of a cross (actually two Greek letters χ and ρ blended together to resemble a cross) and the words under it supposedly read 'in this sign conquer'. He interpreted this as a token from God and vowed that if he won, he would become a Christian. Before the fighting commenced, he ordered his soldiers to paint the cross on their shields. During the fighting, Maxentius drowned in the Tiber and Constantine triumphed. Constantine became the supreme Augustus over all the empire in 312 and reigned a quarter of a century until his death in 337. Throughout history, he became known as Constantine the Great.

Constantine's triumph led to the second event — his conversion to Christ and Christianity. He kept his promise to God to become a Christian and his embracing Christianity had far-reaching effects upon the world, even to this day. Whether he was genuinely converted, we do not know. Due to his vacillation on certain cardinal teachings of Scripture, many question whether his conversion to Christianity was for political expediency or out of personal conviction. In addition, he was not baptized until a few days before his death, by an Arian bishop.

This led to the third event — the Edict of Milan in 313. During his reign, Diocletian ordered what is known as the 'Great Persecution' against Christians and the Church. When Constantine became a professing Christian, all formal persecution ended. However, something positive needed to be enacted. A summit was held in Milan between Emperor Constantine and Licinius, the Caesar of the East. They agreed to give freedom of religion to all, and to recognize the legal status of all Christian churches. An imperial law was passed, but to call it an edict is really a misnomer because no formal edict was ever officially issued. Subsequently, this summit allowed all properties of the churches to be returned and marked the triumph of Christianity over persecution. However, this law did not make Christianity the state religion, as some mistakenly think. The purpose of the summit was to grant toleration and religious freedom to all. It was a major milestone in the history of Christianity.

Since the emperor was now a professed Christian and Christianity was no longer illegal, the fashionable and, for many, the politically expedient thing to do was to convert to Christianity. Many flocked to the church, not because they had truly been reborn, but because it was now popular. Fashionable Christianity has always been the blight of biblical Christianity. The contagious flame of devotion to Christ, holiness of life distinguished from the world, sacrificial service to fellow believers, and the spread of the message of salvation in Christ alone were slowly lost in the milieu of a trendy Christianity.

To combat the seemingly overwhelming growth of the Christian Church, a pagan named Photinius (205–270) set out to check (and hopefully checkmate) its progress. A devout follower of Plato, he formulated Neo-Platonism, a religious revamping of Plato's philosophy. Photinius' twofold aspiration was that Christians would come to their senses and abandon their religion, and that pagans would not convert to it. Photinius would be assisted much later in his war against Christianity by the fall of Rome in 410. Pagans contended that since Rome had abandoned the gods and turned to Christianity, the gods had abandoned Rome. The pagans vigorously proclaimed that Rome's sacking by Alaric, the king of the Visigoths, was the gods' punishment upon it.

Flavius Claudius Julianus (332–363) or Julian the Apostate, as he is more commonly known throughout history, was the nephew of Constantine the Great and grew up as a Christian. He converted to Neo-Platonism and quickly became a militant pagan. Crowned emperor in 360, he initiated a campaign to diminish Christianity and re-establish the heathen worship of the ancient gods. He began by ordering that Christian doctrine be replaced with pagan philosophy in all imperial schools. He rescinded the legal and financial privileges afforded to Christians, even inflicting severe punishments on some who would not renounce their faith. Intending to foster division within the church, Julian allowed all exiled bishops, heretical and orthodox, to return to their sees (the official seat or throne where a bishop ruled over a sphere of churches). He loved to laugh at the divisions and squabbles reported among the various Christian churches. The churches of Asia Minor (especially Syrian Antioch) strongly, but prayerfully, opposed Julian.

Just over two years into Julian's reign, in June of 363, something happened that most Christians interpreted as an act of the almighty hand of God. Using Antioch as the empire's military base in its war with the Persians, Julian launched a fresh campaign against them. In a fierce battle, the apostate was hit by a Persian arrow and mortally wounded. He was immediately taken to Antioch and died that night. Though believed to be slightly embellished, Theodoret (393–466), a Christian historian who was raised in Antioch and knew those who saw the emperor die, claimed that Julian's last words were 'Thou hast conquered, Galilean!' The attempt to overthrow Christianity failed miserably. Jovian (332–364), a supporter of orthodox Christianity, was crowned emperor, and Christianity became fashionable again. These events impacted the church and shaped the world into which John was born.

Two cities

John was born in the city of Antioch on the Orontes River in present-day Syria. Initially, Antioch was the third most important city of the Roman Empire, behind Rome and Alexandria, respectively. It was smaller than Rome and comparable to Alexandria. Situated at the crossroads of land and sea trade routes extending to the far shores of the Mediterranean to the east, Rome to the west, and Egypt to the south, it was a wealthy city. However, all things were not equal; its inhabitants were either enviably rich or tragically poor, with a minority being middle class.

Religiously, there was a mixture of pagans (the resort shrine of Daphne was nearby) and an influential segment of Jews, but Christianity was the controlling influence of the city. Its citizens proudly recalled that the apostles Peter and Paul had both worked at Antioch, and that it was there, according to Acts 11:26, that believers had been first called

Christians. Of course, Paul was sent on his first missionary journey from there (Acts 13:1-5) and tradition holds that Peter was a bishop there before going to Rome. In spite of the dominance of the Christian Church, Antioch was thoroughly Hellenistic in culture, and had statues of pagan gods and goddesses in public areas. Zeus' temple still stood and traditional pagan ceremonies and festivals were held seasonally. As a result, rivalling religious tensions existed. John's response to some of these tensions has caused some historians to misjudge him harshly.

In order to centralize the control of his empire, Constantine the Great shifted his seat of government from Rome to the Greek city of Byzantium in 324. This move replaced Alexandria as the second city in the empire. Byzantium, located on the western shore of the Bosphorus across from Chalcedon, was rebuilt, enlarged, and made Constantine's permanent capital. It was renamed Constantinople (present-day Istanbul) in 330. Elite aristocrats and successful business owners were drafted from other imperial cities by the emperor and relocated in his 'New Rome' to consolidate his purposes. Soon it became a cosmopolitan city of aristocratic politicians, sycophantic courtiers, wealthy businessmen, and favour-seeking bishops, priests and monks. Outwardly, the empire thrived, but inwardly, corruption was widespread.

Alexandria had always felt like a stepchild in the political and, especially, religious arenas. Before the rise of Constantinople, it had been one of the three chief cities of the empire. Three of its most famous citizens, Clement, Origen and Athanasius, gave it just cause to boast. Now it was constantly jousting with Constantinople, Rome, sometimes Antioch, and Jerusalem for significance and primacy. With Constantinople's meteoric rise to prominence, a fierce rivalry ensued between it and Alexandria for political and religious supremacy in the East. Alexandria was the jealous, contriving antagonist. Constantinople's corruption and Alexandria's enmity would play enormous roles in John's later life and ministry. While Alexandria will intrude from time to time, especially at the end, John's story will primarily revolve around Antioch and Constantinople.

Antioch and Constantinople were similar in many ways: Hellenistic (Greek culture and language), a shared economy that was booming throughout the empire, a rich, powerful upper class, an impoverished lower class, and pluralistic tensions. Both had pleasure-seeking reputations because of their fanatical enjoyment of the hippodrome (where horse and chariot races were held) and the theatre. Theatres of John's day were not like modern opera houses or cinema complexes. They were lewd houses of entertainment where actors (usually women immodestly dressed) would perform short plays, sing degenerate tunes, and mouth shameful words. John showed no mercy in his preaching against pleasure seekers in both cities, especially Constantinople.

However, there was one significant difference. Antioch was mainly orthodox (Nicene) and Constantinople was (for the first fifty-plus years of its existence) unorthodox (Arian or Anomoean and semi-Arian). Constantine wavered soon after the Council of Nicaea's declarations and allowed Arians to gain control of the Senate and political entities of Constantinople. When the Nicene orthodox Theodosius I became emperor in 379, there was major political and religious upheaval in the empire's capital. He forbade animal sacrifices to mythological deities, virtually outlawed paganism, made Arianism and other heresies legal offences, and turned complete control of the church and governmental departments over to the Nicene (Trinitarian) orthodox. Arian bishops were deposed or exiled, and replaced with Nicene ones. Arian churches had their presbyters removed and replaced by orthodox pastors. Arians, Anomoeans (the most radical group of Arians), and semi-Arians were not allowed to have their own churches within the city walls of Constantinople. They could live and work there, but not corporately worship there. Yet, they remained latent and subtly became a powerful, disruptive minority, as we will see later.

Two schools

How does one correctly interpret the Holy Bible, not just the Old Testament, but also the New? This simple question has plagued Christians through the centuries. Wars have started, kingdoms have divided and emerged, schismatic groups have formed, and brothers have turned against brothers arguing this question. The Protestant Reformation is a historical product of this troublesome problem. Conflicting views still remain and have engineered the multi-faceted, ecclesiastical structures of present-day Christendom (e.g., Catholic orders, Protestant denominations, and various Christian cults such as the Mormons and Jehovah's Witnesses). Hermeneutics has been defined as the science and art of interpreting Scripture; however, the question still remains: 'How is it done?' In John's day, there were two schools of thought regarding hermeneutical or interpretative principles: allegorical and literal.

Allegory (a literal word, story, or event that is understood in a symbolic way, possessing a deeper meaning) was often used by Jewish exegetes and scholars, especially Philo (*c.* 20 BC – AD 50), who lived in Alexandria. Philo's 'most influential achievement was his development of allegorical interpretation of Scripture which enabled him to discover much of Greek philosophy in the Old Testament, and to combine the respect of his religion for the Pentateuchal law with his personal aspirations towards a more spiritual interpretation of it'. Origen (*c.* 185–254), an early Church Father, biblical critic, exegete and theologian, who also lived in Alexandria, was greatly influenced by Philo and was famous for this method of biblical interpretation.

Though he recognized a triple sense of interpreting and understanding the Scriptures (i. e., literal, moral and allegorical), Origen championed the allegorical. He justified his hermeneutical method on the basis that the whole universe is pervaded with symbols and types of the invisible world. He believed everything seen had a double aspect: one corporal or bodily, and the other spiritual or mystical. This prevailing principle overshadowed his approach to the Holy Bible. This was clearly evident in his preaching, theological writings and commentaries. Alexandria became the ecclesiastical centre for allegorical methodology, and the Alexandrian school of interpretation (as it became known) infected many sectors of Christendom.

The other school of biblical interpretation was grammatical or literal. Emphasis, for this school, lay upon literal, historical and grammatical exegesis that did not allow much typology or spiritualizing. Unlike the Alexandrian school, the Antiochenes did not usually look for the hidden, spiritual or mystical meaning of a text or passage. Instead, they sought the unembellished, intended sense of the inspired writer to his addressees, in its historical setting, with its original purpose. Application could and must come later, but first, the exegete had to determine, via careful historical and grammatical study, the original intent of God through the inspired text. To the literalist, allegory undermined divine inspiration and unlawfully allowed each preacher (or reader) to make the verse or passage say what he wanted it to say. The epicentre of this literal hermeneutic was Antioch, and the Antiochene school of interpretation held sway in several strategic centres of Christendom. Allegorical (Alexandrian) and literal (Antiochene) schools of hermeneutics were in constant conflict. John was born, raised, converted and ordained under the plain-style teaching of the Antiochene discipline, and it fundamentally moulded his entire life and ministry.

2

THE DAYS OF HIS YOUTH

John was born in Antioch of Syria, into a socially respected, middle-class family. Though they were not wealthy, they were financially stable. He was of good Antiochene heritage, although it has been suggested that his father, Secoundus, despite its Greek spelling, was of Latin origin and Roman stock. The year of John's birth has been debated. Some historians date it as early as 344, but internal evidence from his writings and sermons indicate he was most likely born in 349.

Family

His parents were Christians (his mother for certain), though little is known of his father, who probably died when John was young. Despite this, he was not baptized in infancy, which was the practice widely accepted in those days, his family deferred his baptism, and he only took the momentous step of offering himself for it when he was a young man.

Anthousa, his mother, followed the early traditions of the day and never remarried. As a widow, she devoted herself to raising her son and serving Christ in the church. Widowhood was not easy for her. John remembers her as naturally beautiful, but not as flaunting her beauty. In his treatise entitled *On the Priesthood*, John enlarged upon her struggles with borrowing from, but never paying back, family members, unjust tax collectors, and the sacrifices of having to pay for the classical education of her son. She persevered and maintained a strong confidence in her God. Her piety was deep and would be long remembered by John, but it had no saving effect upon him in his early years. Decades later in a sermon, he would quote what one of his academy teachers had said about his mother, also referencing the other godly women of Antioch, 'What remarkable women these Christians have!'

Education

Although any part of John's schooling is inevitably conjectural, Antioch was a famous centre of education, and we may be certain that he received the standard classical Greek education of his day. It was probably in three stages: 1) elementary (age 6–10); 2) grammatical (age 11–14); and 3) rhetorical (age 15–18). The third stage, we are positive, was under the primary tutelage of one of the last and, perhaps, the most distinguished pagan professor and rhetorician, Libanius (314–393). Libanius had also taught Julian the Apostate. The two became personal friends and shared the same disdain for Christianity, but for different reasons. Julian simply hated it, but Libanius feared that Christianity, with its current emphasis on asceticism, would eventually destroy that which was pleasant and beautiful. Therefore, he tenaciously clung to his pagan philosophy to the bitter end.

John revelled and excelled in rhetoric. It came so naturally to him that he caught the special attention of his famous instructor. As Libanius lay dying, his associates asked who should succeed him in the chair of rhetoric. He allegedly replied: 'It ought to have been John had not the Christians stolen him from us.' This early rhetorical training was providentially used of God to form John into the masterful preacher and expositor that he was to become.

Newness of life

When did John come to saving faith in Christ? His star-struck biographer, Palladios, records that John's graduation from the academy coincided with a radical change in his whole mental attitude, and he became absorbed with the Scriptures. Somewhere in the course of his philosophical and rhetorical studies, he became disillusioned and saw the emptiness of the best that man could offer. It is thought that Paul's warning in Colossians 2:8 against pagan philosophy must have significantly influenced John, although there is no substantial proof of it. In his sermons on Colossians, there is a gap between 2:7 and 2:16. It is almost certain he preached from these in-between verses because he alluded to them as he began his homily on 2:16-19. His homily on Colossians 2:8-15 was either not recorded or was lost. It would be interesting to read if there was any reference to his experience in that homily. Nonetheless, we can only speculate as to how Paul's warning against *empty* philosophy affected John. But, somewhere along the way, John became disillusioned with philosophy and started studying the Bible. It was then that he came to repentance and faith in Christ, and throughout the remainder of his life he would call Christianity the true philosophy.

Baptism by immersion

Most converts were required to undertake a two-year catechumenate, in which they studied the great doctrines and practices of the church and were tested on them before being baptized and brought into the church. However, children of Christian parents were considered catechumens from birth (a lesson Christian parents today should take to heart). Thus, John's preparation for baptism was shorter than average, and he was *immersed* (according to the biblical and traditional Greek mode still practised to this day) in all probability, at Easter of the year 368.

Much religious and political turmoil took place between the time of John's birth and his baptism. This turmoil centred primarily on the religious, but when political changes were added to the mix, matters of church and state could never be entirely settled. Just when it seemed that affairs would become normal, another religious or political upheaval would shake up matters again.

The venerable Council of Nicaea in 325 supposedly settled the issue of the Trinity. Simply put, there were basically two groups at Nicaea: the orthodox and the heretical Arians (followers of an Alexandrian priest named Arius, *c.* 256–336). The orthodox were called *homoousians* (meaning of the same essence) and the Arians were called *homoiousians* (meaning of like or similar essence). The difference between these two views may not seem like much (only the small Greek letter *iota* in the spelling), but they were worlds apart. Based upon a faulty exegesis of Colossians 1:15, Arians believed that the Son was inferior to the Father, since the Son was the first thing God created. Thus, the Son was not of the same essence, only of like or similar essence. Nicaea determined the Arians to be heretical and declared the relationship between the Father and the Son to be one and indivisible, of the same essence or substance. For the moment, doctrinal unity was restored to the church. In reality Nicaea's declaration did not settle the issue. Constantine reneged on the very council he summoned, and he allowed exiled Arian and semi-Arian bishops and presbyters to return to their cities and towns. For a while, in certain parts of Christendom, Arianism or semi-Arianism had the upper hand.

Around 360, another controversial and heretical figure emerged named Eunomius, who generated much turmoil in Antioch. His views about Christ were an extreme, radical form of Arianism. His followers were called *anomousians* (meaning of *unlike* or *dissimilar* essence). Along with the standard Arian belief that Christ was the first being God created, Eunomius believed that Christ was of a different substance from God. He also held a strange belief that God was simple in his properties and attributes, and was absolutely intelligible to all. In other words, anyone could understand him, even a non-Christian.

We should acknowledge here that transcendence and immanence, knowability and unknowability, and comprehensibility and incomprehensibility have continually existed as divine tensions in Christian theology. However, when precisely studied, the Scriptures always present a balanced perspective: God is both! The Cappadocian Fathers and John would confront these damnable heresies head on, both in Antioch and Constantinople. Anomoeans (anglicized) had a toehold in Antioch, but a foothold in Constantinople.

As emperors changed, depending on their levels of orthodoxy, so did the religious and political climates. There were three Christian groups in Antioch at the time of John's conversion: the Arians, a large ultra-orthodox congregation led by a presbyter named Paulinus, and the Nicene orthodox led by Meletius. Antioch's beloved Nicene bishop, Meletius, was exiled in 360 and allowed to return in 362. He was exiled again in 367 and allowed to return in 371. This fluctuation, along with other situations in Antioch, created a tattered church community. John witnessed many schisms taking place while growing up. Theodosius I brought an end to the turmoil and secured a more lasting peace throughout the empire when he became emperor in 379, but the bitter strands in Antioch would not be mended until long after John was dead.

Menial service and theological studies

Soon after his baptism, John was taken into close association with Bishop Meletius. He became an executive assistant in episcopal matters, doing mostly the unsung and menial tasks placed upon underlings. During this time, he lived at home with his mother. Seeing the worldliness around him, John desired and decided to practise the ascetic life. This was a strict and rigorous system of practices in which its adherents, both men and women, fought personal sins and strenuously developed soul virtues. The idea, taken from Luke 9:23-26, was to purify the soul and come to love God more perfectly. His mother, having lost her husband, and now with the prospect of losing her son, opposed him. Sharp disagreement ensued between mother and son. They reached a compromise as John agreed to stay home and care for his mother, and his mother agreed to allow John to practise asceticism without joining the communal monks in the desert mountains. Staying at home allowed him to gain valuable experience in matters necessary for a church to function smoothly.

John also had an insatiable hunger to study Holy Scripture, which he read devotedly several times a day. Furthermore, he longed to study theology under Diodore who, along with Flavian, held the orthodox community together and would later become bishop of Tarsas. He enrolled in Diodore's academy and became proficient in theology under his tutelage. John would subsequently proclaim from the pulpit that Diodore was his spiritual father and teacher.

After serving Meletius for approximately three years, John was appointed an official reader or lector, which in the Eastern churches formed the lowest ranking among the clergy, which was immediately below the deacons. This required of him the specific functions of publicly reading the Old Testament lesson and the New Testament epistle at divine liturgy (worship), along with other lesser functions in the administration of the church belonging to the official body of the clergy. Further pressure was put upon him when Emperor Valens, a semi-Arian, took up a short residence in Antioch and Bishop Meletius, a strong *homoousian*, was forced into exile to his homeland of Armenia. Reports were circulating that church authorities were planning to pressgang John and his best friend Basil, not to be confused with 'the Great' of Cappadocia, and ordain them as priests. Both felt unworthy; nevertheless, they agreed to ordination. John, by his own admission, experienced a profound sense of his own worthlessness, and tricked Basil into being ordained while he hid to escape holy orders. John vaguely repented of his trickery, but the deed was already done. He would explain and justify himself in his treatise *On the Priesthood.* The whole convoluted event, which is a story in itself, is still used by his detractors and is a small embarrassment to John's admirers. However, burning within John was a desire to love his Saviour unreservedly and to be more inwardly and eminently holy. He continued serving as a reader of Holy Scripture in divine worship, but that did not satisfy the young man, whose piety was becoming obvious and evident to everyone.

3

MONASTICISM AND
MINISTERIAL ORDINATION

From the time he finished the academy, John and Basil determined to give themselves to the *ascetic* life and avoid worldly excitements. Asceticism was extremely popular among Christians in the second and third centuries of the church's history and was considered by many as the highest level of Christian spirituality and living. The implementation of asceticism was on three basic levels: a limited level while at home or work; a more rigorous level in communities of monks or nuns; and the most severe and austere level, in which monks went farther into the high-desert mountains and lived as hermits.

Noisy community

John's growing dissatisfaction with limited asceticism at home and his yearning to be more holy finally led him to retreat for seven years into the desert mountains of Syria.

There he joined other ascetic monks to live the secluded life. His ascetic life can be divided into two parts. The first part, which lasted four years, was within a community of other mountain monks. Everything was simple. Their modest clothing consisted of goat or camel skins and coarse cloth, which were uncomfortable, to say the least. Each monk lived in a single cell and slept on straw spread over the bare ground with little covering. Only one meal was taken each day, usually eaten communally in the evening. Days were spent with the single motive of simple devotion to God, and little communication among the monks. Each day began with the assembled group reading Scripture and singing psalms in unison and, upon completion of these acts of worship, returned to their cells for intense personal study of the Scriptures. While each had chores to do, such as ploughing and planting, weaving coarse cloth, making baskets to sell, copying books, and occasionally receiving and entertaining visitors, generally the rule of silence was strictly observed. Scholars have noted that these simple rules formed the basis of medieval monasticism.

Solitary man

John became dissatisfied with communal asceticism, feeling that there was too much commotion around the community. Many in the outside Christian world viewed monks as spiritual superstars. Visitors enamoured with the monks frequently came to observe communal life and interact with them. John believed that the noisy coming and going of people, trafficking as he considered it, disturbed his drawing closer to God. So, he withdrew farther into the mountains where he engaged in a more rigorous regimen. These last three years marked the second part of his ascetic life. He was primarily alone and, as a result, he ate little, fasted often, and severely neglected his body. Neo-Platonism still shaded this aspect of his thinking. It was here that he endeavoured to memorize the entire Bible, both the Old and New Testaments. Little did John realize that this strenuous activity would prove to be the most profitable of all his ascetic practices. Eventually, his body could take no more. Austere and spartan living finally broke his health and he was forced to return to Antioch. John bodily left the ascetic life, but in his soul he remained a monk for ever. He would live frugally and give his money to the church and to the sick and poor all his days. This frugality would one day be used against him at his deposition trial, as will be seen later.

The death of Emperor Valens signalled the collapse of the Arian interpretation of Scripture, brought Meletius back to Antioch, and induced John's ordination into the diaconate, the rank of Christian ministry immediately under the priesthood. During this period of service John, still not licensed to preach, busied himself writing treatises and pamphlets. His writings covered a wide range of subjects, such as the person and power of Christ, repentance and suffering, celibacy, marriage and sexual purity, educating children and new converts, the priesthood, monasticism (which always lay close to his heart), the evils of pederasty (paedophilia), theatregoing, horse racing, the cult of the Manichees, and the superfluous luxuries of the rich who professed Christ. Three elements woven throughout are apparent in his writings: his love and devotion to Christ; his fervent communion with the triune God; and a strong desire for true, gospel holiness and piety.

Presbyterial ordination

Upon the death of Meletius, Flavian (a strong Nicene) was
consecrated bishop of Antioch. In the opening weeks of
386, Flavian ordained John into the priesthood. For almost
twelve quiet and mostly uneventful years (386–398), John
laboured contentedly in Antioch. The years of solitary
study and memorization in the monastic caves gave him an
exceptional mastery of the Bible. After he began to preach,
his reputation as a solid expositor and plain-style preacher of
the Holy Scriptures quickly grew, and multitudes thronged
to hear him. John was given the largest and most beautiful
church building in Antioch and almost always preached in
the bishop's cathedral during Flavian's absence. It was during
this period that John delivered his homilies on the books of
Genesis, Matthew, John, Romans, Corinthians, Galatians,
Ephesians, Timothy and Titus. His down-to-earth sermons,
based upon his Antiochene hermeneutic, drew vast crowds
that were eager to hear him. Greek icons (delicate, hand-
painted pictures) portrayed John in his mature years as a
diminutive, slightly bald man. However, what he lacked in
physique, he made up in soul and heart. Throughout the
Christian world, John's renown as a brilliant and powerful
expositor of the Holy Scriptures spread.

Controversial preaching

More will be said about John's preaching later, but one
scattered set of homilies preached in Antioch must be
considered now. Due to misunderstanding, these homilies
have been the occasion for controversy and much criticism.

They dealt with Christians participating in Jewish customs and ceremonies. A sizeable and influential community of Jews resided in Antioch. They were wealthy, lived among the general population (not confined to ghettos as has been claimed), had several synagogues in the city and surrounding areas, and were generally liked by the Christian community. Contrary to modern critics, John was not anti-Semitic. He did not hate Jews, but he was greatly disturbed by their public ceremonial practices, especially their Feast of Trumpets, Day of Atonement, and weeklong Feast of Tabernacles. Jewish feasts were only shadows and, like all shadows, must give way to the light. What was more disturbing to John than the Jews' public festivals was the Christian participation in their festivals and superstitious beliefs regarding the Jews. Many Christians, attracted by ancient pageantry, thought that joining in the Jewish public feasts would make them more holy. Many also thought it would bring *good luck* to be associated with a Jew or have an oath or business transaction officially ratified in a synagogue. Others thought consulting a rabbi when sick would help them get well sooner. It was such childish behaviour and superstition on the part of Christians that motivated John to preach these controversial sermons.

Interspersed throughout the latter part of 386 and all of 387, John interrupted his regular expositions and addressed the issue in seven separate homilies. His homilies were later grouped together and misleadingly entitled *Against the Jews*. Again, for John, the problem was not the Jews themselves; he desired their eternal salvation. In other contexts, he spoke approvingly of them and commended them for obedience to their religion in the face of opposition. Despite his laudable concern for the spiritual salvation of Abraham's physical seed, he needlessly used harsh words and sharp rhetorical invectives in these sermons. His sincere intent and hope was to correct his erring sheep pastorally. John's primary angst in these sermons was against the Christians who intermingled Judaism with Christianity. Opponents have accused John of fostering anti-Semitic attitudes that justified the slaughter of millions of Jews in the twentieth century. This was not the case. Since the Jews evicted the first Christians from their synagogues in the early chapters of the Book of Acts, the church had purposefully sought to maintain a clear distinction between the old and the new Israel (e.g., Romans 2:28-29; Galatians 6:16). Existing literature reveals that John was a product of his time and no different than his contemporaries.

Famous preaching

One other event during John's ministry in Antioch would gain him empire-wide attention: the citizens' riot against the emperor and John preaching twenty-one homilies entitled *On the Statues*. The incident started three days before Lent (forty days of self-denial before Easter).

On 27 February 387, a large crowd was gathered outside the courthouse to hear an imperial proclamation that had just arrived. When the edict was read, the crowd was hushed in stunned silence. The emperor, under financial hardship, levied an exorbitant tax upon the city of Antioch, the province's capital. Common opinion was that the Antiochenes were already heavily strained to pay present taxes, and additional taxation would, indeed, break them. Among those in the crowd were hired professionals, paid by politicians and actors to applaud vigorously their personages in parades or on stage. John disdainfully called these hirelings 'strangers and foreigners'. Suddenly, the silence was ended by women starting to wail. The crowd immediately erupted into a mad fury, driven by the professional applauders. For whatever reason, they rushed to the bathhouses of Caligula, smashing everything in their way. After they demolished the bathhouses, the mob turned back to the praetorium and forced their way inside to the great, marbled audience hall. Their intent was to demand of the prefect the abrogation of the announced tax. The prefect was nowhere to be found. Hearing the riotous noise, the official slipped over the wall outside the city to search for imperial troops.

Meanwhile, inside the praetorium, the frustrated and nearly exhausted mob was ready to give up and return to their homes. Then, as folklore tells it, a small boy holding a stone in his hand suddenly flung it at the statue of Emperor Theodosius sitting on a horse. This defiant act revived the mob and they gathered rocks and began throwing them at all the statues of the imperial family. These statues represented everything the seditionists hated. Altogether, there were five bronze-covered statues, representing the Emperor Theodosius, his recently deceased wife Flacilla, the emperor's father, Count Theodosius, and the emperor's two sons Honorius and Arcadius. The mob overturned the statues, defaced and mangled them. By then it was raining and, not to be deterred, the mob carried the mutilated statues through the muddy streets in self-deluded victory. It was reported that the frenzied rabble chanted slurs at the statue of the mounted Theodosius and challenged him to defend himself now.

Approximately three hours later, the prefect entered the city with imperial soldiers (mostly archers) and dispersed the riotous crowds. All that remained of the infamous riot was twisted pieces of bronze statues in the muddy streets; no suspension of the levy, only a deathly silence over the great city. Slowly dawning upon the minds of everyone in Antioch was the realization that they had just committed the greatest and most unpardonable of all state crimes — high treason. The penalty, as everyone knew, was death. Praetorian guards immediately began rounding up the suspected leaders of the riot, especially the professional applauders, and summarily executed several of them. City-government officials and leading citizens were taken hostage and cross-examined in torture chambers. Their properties and wealth were confiscated, and the wives and children of those arrested were put out of their homes. Punishment had begun. Rumours flew around the city that the emperor would order the annihilation of all inhabitants and raze the metropolis to the ground. Many of the rich, almost all the pagan philosophers, and, to the embarrassment of Libanius, most of his students fled to the high-desert mountains of Syria. All bathhouses, theatres and the hippodrome were closed down. Executions were carried out for days. John tells us: 'There is a silence, huge with terror, and loneliness everywhere.' Fear gripped the people. What would they do?

Knowing the wrath of the emperor, Bishop Flavian (now eighty years old) secretly left the city and travelled an eight-hundred-mile journey through blustery snow to Constantinople to plead with Theodosius for mercy. Those who knew of the mercy pilgrimage did not believe the old bishop would survive the punishing journey, much less succeed in his intercession with the mighty emperor. There appeared to be no hope. John observed the executions and remained silent for several days, but his spirit so burned within him that he could no longer contain himself. What would he do in this time of great crisis? John did what any man called of God would do: he mounted the pulpit and preached the Word of God. He reminded the people that this was all God's doing to strip them of every earthly comfort, to humble them to seek him, not only during this time of crisis, but all the days of their lives, and to better fit them for heaven. He comforted, rebuked, exhorted, directed, and gave praise to God, using all his rhetorical skills. In his last of these sermons, John even praised the people for their contrition and repentance. Since all the public entertainment centres were shut down, the church was filled to capacity at each sermon; even pagans came to hear him.

As an imperial army drew near to Antioch, fear heightened. Mysteriously, hermit monks from the mountains showed up and began going through the streets interceding for those about to be executed. One aged monk named Macedonius, in tattered garments and barefooted, grabbed the bridle of his horse and entreated Caesarius, a court prefect and commander of the dispatched troops, to show mercy to the people as Christ had shown mercy to him and the emperor. Such was the respect that Caesarius and the troops had for these holy men that everyone dismounted and kneeled as they listened to the monk's passionate plea. When John learned that the monks' caves were then filled with many of Antioch's richest citizens and almost all its philosophers and scholars, he laid his invective on them in the next homily:

Tell me this: Where are those long-bearded fellows — those cynical lickers-up-of-crumbs-from-below-the-table, those gentlemen who work so hard on behalf of their bellies? I will tell you! They have scurried away and hidden themselves in the caves and dens of our hermits who walk boldly about our forum as though no calamity had ever threatened.

Scholars are divided over the exact days and dates when each of John's homilies *On the Statues* was delivered, but they probably commenced seven days after the sedition occurred. Mounting the pulpit in the bishop's cathedral, John engaged his divinely-bestowed powers of preaching, producing what some historians consider his most admirable sermons. It was John's direct and powerful expositions that brought calm, birthed humility and repentance, and restored sanity to a frenzied and later fearful population. Theodosius did yield to the pleas of the godly Flavian. The city was spared and its exalted status was returned.

Preached in an intense atmosphere of stress and fear, these homilies amply confirmed John's position as Antioch's leading preacher and that he was already master of the art of the political sermon.

Picking up the pen

Preserved for us is a large body of John Chrysostom's writings. There are more written works of his than any of the other Greek Fathers. Having received outstanding rhetorical training under Libanius, John was able to transfer that skill, to a sufficient degree, from mouth to pen. His output is so prolific and extensive, covering not only expositions of whole books of the Bible, but topics so relevant that they could have been preached yesterday. His literature has been so esteemed through the centuries that they have been translated into many languages and, as more scientific knowledge of ancient Attic Greek is acquired, scholars are retranslating his works to gain a better and clearer understanding of what he wrote and spoke.

Excluding his sermons, most of his writing took place during the period after he returned from his ascetic life and before his ordination as a presbyter. Serving as an assistant to Bishop Flavian, he had extra time on his hands, so he busied himself as a pamphleteer, a writer of pamphlets or booklets. His earlier writings were repetitious and somewhat bumbling. Like any novice writer, the more he wrote the more competent he became. Most of his writings were apologetic and pastoral treatises. Noteworthy among his publications are *On St. Babylas against Julian and the Pagans* (Babylas was the defiant bishop of Antioch, who was martyred *c.* 250); *Against Jews and Pagans on the Divinity of Christ* (which trumpets the active power of Christ as the reason for the demise of each and victory of Christianity over both); *Contrition of Heart* (which stresses the Christian's continual need to maintain a humble and repentant heart, constantly warring against remaining sin, and always burning with a fervent love for Christ); *To Stageirius* (which addresses the problem of human suffering and God's hand of providence in it); *Virginity* (which extols the ideals of this state and the necessity to maintain moral and sexual purity); *To a Young Widow* (which comforts and instructs a noble lady whose husband had suddenly died); and *Single Marriage* (where, following the custom of his day, he praises the idea of remaining a widow and serving Christ the remainder of her days).

Two of his writings show a strain of brilliance that reflects John's heart throughout his ministry: *A King and a Monk Compared* and *To Theodore When He Fell Away*. The former was John's defence of the ascetic/monastic life. The king may command powerful armies, but the monk has access to the God who commands even kings. The king may have the riches of the world, but the monk has the greater riches of the world to come. This present, temporary world, that shall surely pass away, is not all that there is to life; there is an everlasting world to come, and it shall never end. When the dust has finally settled, the monk is far more blessed and vastly superior to a king. The latter is to a close friend, Theodore, who had joined the ascetic life with John, but soon turned away because of family business and desires for marriage. The eloquence of the treatise was considered by many at the time to be almost more divine than human as he pleaded with Theodore to flee his fleshly desires and turn his gaze to heaven where Christ would rescue him and grant him greater significance and meaning to life. The treatise had its desired effect, and Theodore renounced his worldly pursuits and returned to Christ's service. Theodore later became a brilliant theologian and Bishop of Mopsuestia. He is also reputed to have sat in the second great ecumenical at Constantinople in 381.

As one reads John's works, the heart of the preacher is quickly seen. He was a man of high emotions and holy passions and, in his writings like his preaching, he sought to state his position, develop and argue it using every rhetorical method possible, and conclude by silencing every potential objection. Among his surviving works are over eight hundred sermons, which were mostly taken down by shorthand. Within those that survived, there are references to other sermons that are not extant, which confirms suspicion that a number were lost. His sermons on the Acts of the Apostles are the only surviving commentary on that New Testament book available from the first one thousand years of Christian history. Also, over two hundred personal letters exist, some official and others personal. Though references to himself are made in his personal correspondence, they are mostly given over to helping, teaching, correcting and encouraging his addressees.

4

BISHOP OF CONSTANTINOPLE

Constantinople was not only the luxurious city of the world for pagans, but also the holy city of God for eastern Christianity. The emperor was not only the head of the empire, but also the earthly head of the church and, as such, had to walk an extremely fine line to keep harmony between the two, despite the fact that the empire was officially Christian. Sometimes the Christians acted in such a manner that one could not distinguish them from pagans, and sometimes, pagans surprisingly acted with more grace and integrity than the Christians. Sad, indeed, were the comparisons!

It has been stated that the second half of the fourth century was a turbulent time. Christianity struggled to gain a foothold against competing religions, as increasingly it came to exert its influence. Just as often, Christian group fought against Christian group for power and influence. This statement vividly describes Constantinople upon John's arrival.

Before the death of Theodosius the Great, the last sole ruler of the empire, in 395, he appointed his two sons to succeed him to the throne. The younger, Honorius (384–423), was given the Western Empire centred in Rome and the older, Arcadius (377–408), was given the Eastern Empire centred in Constantinople. Like their father, both were staunch Nicene orthodox. Arcadius, the emperor directly related to John and our story, was only eighteen years old when he ascended the Eastern throne. Therefore, a trusted general named Rufinus was appointed guardian-counsellor for the young emperor. Arcadius was small-framed, had drooping eyes, stammered or stuttered when he spoke, was intellectually dull and sluggish, weak in character, driven by sensual propensities, and one who could and would be easily manipulated. Aelia Eudoxia, his exceptionally charming and beautiful wife, was just the opposite. The daughter of a Frank general, she had grown up watching powerful men in action. She was vivacious, extroverted, intelligent and witty, perceptive, manipulative, strong-willed, ambitious, impulsive, very superstitious, and, at times, volatile. Seeing the weakness in her emperor husband, she quickly gained control of the marriage and, eventually, became the shadow ruler of the empire. On 9 January 400, Eudoxia was proclaimed Augusta and from that point on she is always pictured wearing the imperial insignia of a diadem (crown), which only a reigning emperor or empress could wear.

Is there a bishop around?

The Council of Constantinople in 381 decreed that the Bishop of Constantinople be given primacy and honour next to the Bishop of Rome. Nectarius, the Bishop of Constantinople who replaced Gregory Nazianzus at the Council of Constantinople in 381, died in 397. Who would replace him as the next bishop? The answer was of immeasurable importance. One requirement was non-negotiable: the new bishop must be a Nicene orthodox. Much heated and wide-ranging discussion was held at the imperial court. Several possible candidates were considered as unabashed lobbying was utilized. Lobbyists (yes, they existed in that day!) cleverly plied their richly-paid skills vetting each client's qualified candidate. One client in particular, who would play a dark role in the drama of the next seven years, was Theophilus, the powerful, ambitious and unscrupulous patriarch of Alexandria. He strongly lobbied for an aged priest named Isidore in the Alexandrian church. Theophilus planned indirectly to control the old man, who had recently turned eighty, and garner additional influence in the empire. Isidore was rejected, and Theophilus became furious.

While numerous court officials and local church leaders were involved in the selection process, canonical law stated that only the emperor, as the head of the church, could make the final choice. Canonical law must be strictly followed. Arcadius, indecisive and easily manipulated, was heavily influenced by Eutropius, his secretary of state. Bypassing all potential candidates, Emperor Arcadius looked to the Syrian metropolis of Antioch for his new bishop. The court had drawn from this spiritual well in the past and, now, it would do so again. John was chosen to become the twelfth Bishop of Constantinople.

Why was John chosen?

Before considering how John was tricked, kidnapped, and
clandestinely taken to Constantinople, thought must be
given as to why he was chosen, above all of the potential
candidates. There are several possible reasons. Firstly, his
fame as an expository preacher of the Scripture, possessing
great eloquence and erudition, had grown virtually
throughout the empire. There were few who had not heard
of him. On one occasion, while on state business, Eutropius
visited Antioch and heard John preach. The emperor's
chamberlain immediately discerned that here was a man of
genuine moral and spiritual integrity. Secondly, the direct
and calming pastoral leadership which he had demonstrated
during the Antiochian riot of 387 was noticed by Caesarius,
who was now a consul. He had been commander of the
troops and one of the imperial negotiators in that city during
the event. It was John's strength of character, Caesarius
observed, that kept the city calm and prevented further riots
or reprisals against the troops. Thirdly, his zeal for Nicene
orthodoxy was impeccable. The Theodosian court wanted
someone who was not afraid to vigorously confront the
Anomoeans and semi-Arians in Constantinople. At this time,
the Arian minority was in a distinctly militant mood, and
John was correctly assumed to be the man for the job. John
had a proven track record of success in boldly and mightily
opposing the Anomoeans in public debate and diminishing
their numbers. Why could he not do so again? Fourthly, the
bureaucrats of the 'New Rome' desired someone who would
advance their political agenda and broaden the authority
of the imperial see. Rome, because the apostles Paul and
Peter had been martyred there, claimed primacy over all

the other sees. Constantinople wanted to sway religious opinion and seize Rome's primacy. A number of imperial counsellors believed that John could help bring this to pass. However, it remains unknown whether John was chosen for one or a combination of all the above reasons. Whatever the reason(s), John was God's providential choice and history was made.

How can we get him here?

The Christians in Antioch delighted in the preaching of John and deeply loved him. Many had either been converted or had grown spiritually under his ministry. How would the court get John out of Antioch and into Constantinople without causing another political uproar? A clever plan was devised requiring the quiet and deceitful cooperation of several government officials. In late October 397 (probably in mid-afternoon), an urgent summons from the governor of the district of the Orontes arrived at John's church office. The order was for John to leave immediately and meet the governor at the great martyrs' shrine located outside the Romanesian Gate. It was probably early evening when John arrived. Without any explanation, John was put into a coach and driven fifteen miles away from the city. Night had fallen. The emperor had given the governor strict orders to dispatch this matter with utmost secrecy. Riding in the coach, the governor then broke the overpowering news that John had been chosen to be the next bishop of Constantinople, and that he was being taken there, under imperial orders, for his consecration into the office. Thus, under the cover of night for fear that the people of the city and the congregations of their deeply loved preacher would riot, John was quietly snatched out of Antioch and taken to Constantinople. Scholars think this action was against John's will; nevertheless, he quietly submitted to his emperor's order. Bishop Flavian, no doubt, had advanced notice of what transpired but kept the secret to himself. It took several weeks for John to arrive at the capital.

As the imperial entourage slowly travelled to Constantinople, Emperor Arcadius convened a special synod of leading bishops throughout Christendom. His purpose was formally to solemnize and consecrate his new bishop. The emperor wanted to highlight the solemnity of the occasion and to further the special status of the imperial see. From the time of the summons until they arrived in Constantinople, all the bishops were kept in suspense as to who the next bishop of this 'New Rome' would be. Upon arriving, many probed officials and slowly discovered that the imperial choice was John of Antioch. Theophilus, rather than submitting to the will of God and desiring God's blessings upon his chosen servant, became even more furious. He did everything within his power to oppose the emperor's decision and to have Arcadius withdraw his choice of John. He even instigated a slanderous smear campaign against John's name and reputation. He was not successful. Threatened by court officials, especially Eutropius, to cease and desist, Theophilus backed away from his opposition to John. Theophilus was then manipulated into chairing the council that formally recognized and consecrated John as the new bishop. Nonetheless, instead of repenting, the bitter and vengeful Theophilus became a lifelong enemy of John, opposing him until the bitter end. On 26 February 398, John Chrysostom was ordained and consecrated the twelfth bishop of Constantinople. Though John had ecclesiastical authority over a host of bishops and was often called archbishop, it should be carefully noted here that the title of archbishop, which was often mistakenly attributed to him, was not in use at the see of Constantinople until the Council of Chalcedon in 451.

Toil

Though some can read of John's labours and ministry as bishop and receive hope and encouragement, most will not. It should have been the best of days for John, wherein he should have exercised a profitable ministry and spent the remainder of his life filled with visionary prospects for the advancement of the gospel. The first few months in Constantinople were obviously an encouragement for him. However, elation at receiving a new bishop, renowned for his piety, careful exegesis, and Christ-centred preaching, disappeared like a flash. It appears, almost from the start, that this holy and faithful preacher of Christ and his Word fought a long, uphill battle which culminated with him being deposed.

John was a reformer at heart and when he ascended the throne of bishop, he found the church there in disarray. The former bishop, as he had grown older, had lost his zeal for a holy church and his vision for gospel expansion. He became swallowed up in many luxuries the metropolitan city had to offer. What was scandalous to John was that his predecessor often held lavish state dinners and galas, even for minor dignitaries and prelates. (John's ascetic mindset would not allow him to indulge in such outlandish behaviour. Occasionally, he would host a state dinner, as the need required, but not with the lavishness of Nectarius. This would later be used against him.) John set out to remedy the maladies of a sick and weakened church. Situations would change rapidly.

The new bishop's first reform was upon the clergy. John had ecclesiastical oversight and guidance over large portions of Europe and Asia. There were, at least, twenty-eight bishops under his widespread authority and almost ten thousand presbyters, clerics and church administrative workers in the city of Constantinople alone, which had a population of over one hundred thousand. His pastoral responsibilities were enormous. Because his predecessor had set the pattern, John quickly discovered that many of his clergy were lazy, accustomed to living in luxury, and sumptuously wined and dined under the guise of hospitality. After all, were they not in the political and spiritual capital of the empire? Must they not keep up appearances? Few of the clergy genuinely cared about the spiritual well-being of their parishioners, much less the sick and poor. Also, there abounded a peculiar custom (as John saw it) among the celibate priests, whereby single women moved into the priests' homes and became live-in housekeepers. The priests preferred to call them spiritual sisters. John, who understood the sinfulness of human nature, knew better. Instead of these spiritual sisters freeing up the pastors from menial household tasks so they could give themselves more fully to the work of the gospel, the custom incited sexual immorality and produced many illegitimate children. Nameless orphans running around the streets of Constantinople gave concrete proof of this fact.

John began his reform with the clergy in reverse order. He called in all the spiritual sisters and gave each a private interview. No doubt, he instructed them on the necessity of maintaining sexual purity and warned them of failure and its consequences. Then, without mincing any words, the bishop preached two stinging sermons to his clergy and their housekeepers against this practice. He noted that spiritual sisters oftentimes became spiritual mothers. How could a bishop (referring to his predecessor) tolerate such a custom? A bishop who would allow such was worse than a panderer. This custom had to be abolished. Needless to say, this did not make the carnal-minded happy.

Next, John set out to reform and establish a godly ministry in the churches. He did this by interviewing and assessing each priest, which took a considerable amount of time. He then assigned godly and faithful pastors to strategic churches, and he charged them to become true ministers of the Word and shepherds of their flocks. After determining who the unfaithful clerics were, he reassigned them to tedious administrative tasks in the cathedral and other menial, diocesan duties. These attempts at reformation brought acquiescence from the men of God but little change of heart from the hirelings.

The new bishop then turned his attention to reforming the finances of the church. John realized that no records had been kept and no accounting of moneys had been demanded. His predecessor had been too busy luxuriously feasting and fawning over the politicos of the capital to care. John would have none of this. He began keeping a record book of all money received and spent, cut off large sums of income to church custodians and stewards, reduced funds used on frivolous catering to the rich and famous, demanded receipts for every penny spent, and expected a clear balance-sheet periodically. It is interesting to note at this point that John saved enough church money within the first year to build a new hospital.

Part of the responsibility that fell under John's ecclesiastical administration was the oversight and maintenance of charitable institutions such as poor-houses, hospitals and orphanages. He loved the poor, and wisely used church money to build them hospitals. He cared deeply for the orphans (many of whom were the illegitimates of nobles, wealthy politicians and even priests), and he built many orphanages for them. He often pleaded their plight to the rich in his sermons. Several times the commoners and poor people rocked the entire capital in support of their bishop. Fear of the people restrained the emperor and the imperial court from taking actions against John on numerous occasions.

Furthermore, to raise the level of godliness and spirituality in the city, he ordered the churches to be opened at night so that any day-workers who desired it could partake in soul-strengthening devotions after work. There would be singing of the Psalms, reading of Holy Scripture, a short devotional homily and prayers. This meant that the ministers would have extra duties to perform. Again, there was grumbling.

While there were a few good and godly presbyters loyal to Christ who welcomed his arrival and enthronement as bishop, most resented John's pastoral interruption of their fleshly pleasures and his new impositions. A rebellion among the priests against their bishop's new orders soon exploded. John swiftly suspended and probably excommunicated the ringleaders and forbade the Lord's Supper to the rest of the rebels. By the end of six months, the majority of the priests were simmering with insubordination and complaints. Nevertheless, John was the bishop, and his word was church law. He would not back down, and he was more determined than ever to have a godly ministry in his bishopric. Unless the emperor intervened, there was nothing the priests could do. Eventually, matters calmed down, but the resentment among the hirelings did not. Several who nursed long, venomous grudges would later bring false charges against John.

Trouble

Immediately, as we have seen, many factors worked against the success of this principled exegete and bishop. The main factor was that John entered a city that was more Christian in name than in essence. Its inhabitants were carried away with court matters and politics, lavish banquets and feasts, drunkenness, going to theatres and chariot races in the hippodrome (especially on Sundays), acquiring wealth and treasures, purchasing high-fashioned clothes and jewelry, building, tearing down, and rebuilding mansions and holiday villas. John was grieved that more money was spent on these things than giving to the work of Christ's kingdom and the sick and the needy who were drawn to the capital hoping to find mercy and help. Spiritual vitality was extremely low. Religious enthusiasm peaked on saints' days, Christmas and Easter, but quickly evaporated with the passing of these occasions. Though many of the people gave lip-service to Christianity, and there was a godly seed present, most were governed by their affections for the pleasures of this world.

It was not long before John began to address these matters in his expositions, just as he had done in Antioch.

As it has always been, fashionable Christianity will resist and soon chafe under Christ-centred preaching on holiness, denying oneself, and sacrificing for the kingdom of God. John reminded his hearers that there was someone greater than themselves, and that there was a greater kingdom than their own. He called them to account and warned of failed or delayed obedience. His preaching was not well received by most of the higher-ups. His homilies against worldliness and self-centredness generated their ire and innuendoes.

The imperial court was stunned at John's rapid reforms. To say the least, John had more about him than they had anticipated. Everyone in the imperial court had expected a compliant bishop who would spontaneously yield to their promptings, enhance the prestige of the imperial see by outshining Rome, win over or at least silence the boisterous and heretical Arians, and generally make the people happy and satisfied. After all, had he not captured the hearts of the city of Antioch? Had he not accomplished things that bordered on the miraculous? Was not John the best orator in Christendom? Instead, they were shaken out of their lethargy to discover that they had a real man of God on their hands, one who could not be controlled. The most important question was yet to be asked. How would the emperor and his domineering wife respond?

Emperor Arcadius, who respected but feared John, was personally too weak to do anything. As long as matters did not disturb his comfort zone, he was content to stay quietly in the background and indulge his sensual privileges, which only a monarch could have. Only reluctantly did he emerge to take action in John's life and ministry as he was forced either by circumstances beyond his control or by his domineering wife. He was a despicable figure indeed!

Eudoxia, Arcadius' imperious, tempestuous, and most likely immoral wife, was another matter. It was rumoured that Eudoxia had liaisons with a courtier named Count John. She would play a starring role in the tragic drama of John's ministry in Constantinople. Although it has been claimed that she was a deeply superstitious Christian, one can only wonder. Eudoxia had a love-hate relationship with John, which increasingly slid towards loathing. At first, she ardently supported John and spent many hours talking and perhaps discussing theology with him. She had John baptize her son. When the bishop appealed for money to buy ornate silver crosses, which he believed were needed to counter the Saturday nocturnal processions of the Anomoeans, Eudoxia donated the total amount for their purchase. She even joined the bishop, without her royal attire and barefooted, on a midnight, torchlight procession through the city in which the relics of a martyr were carried from the port to the Church of St Thomas, almost seven miles west of the city centre. John praised her for the humility she demonstrated that night in his sermon the next morning. Most of these events took place within the first two years of his ministry in Constantinople when John enjoyed mediocre favour with the court (*c*. 398–400).

John first sensed Eudoxia's displeasure when he defended Eutropius in late 399 (as shall be examined later). Remember, in the capital, John was perpetually surrounded by extravagance and waste. Greed and contriving to obtain more was an acceptable standard. High fashion and flaunting expensive attire were everywhere evident and admired. The race to see who could get the most the fastest never ended. What grieved the heart of this servant of the lowly Nazarene was that there was no embarrassment or humility over such behaviour. Months after Eutropius' fall, while making application in a sermon on greed, John drew the empress' ire. He painted a vivid picture of just a few months previous, how many of his hearers who had kissed the feet of this fallen politician were now fighting over and savagely gorging themselves with his exorbitant possessions. Referring to the flamboyant gold necklaces and chains worn by wealthy ladies in church, he contrasted them with the rude chains worn by Paul in prison. He then pointed a finger directly at the empress herself and said that if Paul entered the church in his chains and wounds, with Eudoxia sitting there clad in all her gold and finery, the people would look at the apostle, not the empress. As a strong orthodox professor, she was bound outwardly to assent, but it is certain that she was inwardly angered at the public exposure and comparison. In another sermon, John garnered more displeasure from Eudoxia by explaining that true beauty was of the heart and not in outward appearances. He spoke of 'these gaudy Jezebels, with their trinkets, their false hair, and their paste' trying to cover up age and faded beauty. Everyone believed John was referring to three prominent court widows, who were very close friends and counsellors of the empress.

John continued his particularly damaging practice of frequently mentioning the excesses of women (expensive and immodest dresses, excessive jewelry, elaborate hair arrangements), usually referencing Jezebel (1 Kings 21:5-16) and Herodias (Matthew 14:1-12). John was not a misogynist, nor did he think that women should look frumpy; but, as a child, his beautiful, yet godly, mother had modelled before him the example of a Christian woman. She was in stride with the styles of her day, nevertheless, she was modest, humble, and never flashy. As a result, he thought all

Christian women should be this way. Believing that he had the exegetical authority of 1 Timothy 2:9 and 1 Peter 3:3-4, John persisted in this. Many thought that John's insinuations were subtly directed toward the empress Eudoxia. So did Eudoxia, as history affirms.

One final clash with the empress became a spike in John's ecclesiastical coffin. The smaller forum of Constantinople had the Holy Wisdom Cathedral to the west and the hippodrome adjacent on the southeast. Between the two was a raised platform that was often used to make special or royal announcements. Eudoxia, ever desirous of attention and praise, had a towering silver statue of herself erected on the platform. Its shadow loomed over the entrance to the church. Furthermore, she had it put in place on a Sunday morning during divine worship. This event was not done quietly, but carried out with all the festivities of a pagan ceremony. The music, the singing, and the roaring applause could be heard in the church and was so loud at times that it drowned out John's preaching. Instead of sending out a deacon and courteously asking for the celebration to be postponed until the worship of God was completed, John lost his temper and began pointedly to address the sinful occasion.

He scathingly denounced the organizers (especially for the timing of it), insisted that the event was an outrage and an insult to the church of Jesus Christ, and that he regarded it as a disgrace to an empress who called herself a Christian. Why were the celebrants not in the house of God adoring the King of heaven, instead of being in the forum of men exalting the empress? John's anger was understandable to those who loved Christ above all others, but not to the carnal-minded, especially those of the imperial household. Eudoxia, so vainly self-centred and self-righteous, was infuriated. News of her outrage came to John in cryptic messages from courtiers. John later exclaims in a sermon: 'once again Herodias is dancing, and seeks the head of John', and in another: 'In the evening she called me the thirteenth apostle, today she branded me as Judas'. In a sermon preached in early May 403, he departed from his standard practice of exposition and vehemently denounced 'the weaknesses conventionally attributed to women'. Several hearers connected the dots to Eudoxia. The imperial court was severely displeased and the empress told Arcadius that she would no longer tolerate John and his preaching. Some scholars have identified this as the fateful turning-point in John's fortunes.

Sycophants (people who tried to win favour by flattery) at the imperial court also played their part in troublemaking. John saw them as existing for their own advancement rather than the glory of Christ and the good of the people. There was incessant haggling and long petty disputes among them. As a spiritual advisor, John was regularly called upon to mediate and settle their quarrels, often to everyone's dissatisfaction. He tired easily and frequently had to rest after sessions of mediating childish senatorial and administrative squabbles — all of which, he believed, robbed him from the work of Christ's glory and kingdom and the salvation of souls. Recurrently mentioning the abuses of wealth and power in his preaching and refusing to partake of the regular social life of the capital offended the ruling class. They considered his humble lifestyle scandalous. Why could John not be like Nectarius? His preaching was often a kill-joy to the courtiers, and he would find no true friend among them.

Then those who should have been his closest allies, namely bishops (who were jealous) and priests (who felt slighted), added their part. Bishops from the rural provinces regularly came into the capital and spent considerable time there enjoying the high life of the metropolis. At any given time, there would be a number of provincial bishops present. Within his first year in office, John had deposed a group of bishops under his authority for financial misappropriations and *simony* (the buying or selling of positions in the church, a term named after Simon Magus in Acts 8:18). He further demanded that all of his bishops and priests come into biblical compliance. They did not understand his zeal to maintain a godly testimony of Christ and his church before a watching and perishing world. Nor did they realize that their ungodly actions quenched the Spirit of God and held back the blessings of heaven upon them. Many resented John's principled actions against them. It seemed, at times, as if John had no friends; however, there was one.

Immediately upon arrival at the bishop's cathedral (the *Hagia Sophia* which means 'Holy Wisdom' in Greek), he was introduced to a woman who was the chief deaconess and head of the convent. Her name was Olympias. She was a granddaughter of one of Constantine's praetorian prefects and was inherently wealthy. Widowed at the age of eighteen, Emperor Theodosius wanted her to marry his nephew. She meekly refused stating that if God had wanted her to be married, he would not have taken away her husband. The emperor became furious and confiscated all her wealth and properties. She wrote a gracious letter to Theodosius thanking him for relieving her of the heavy burden of managing her money. Her only request was that he divided her wealth between the church and the charitable institutions that cared for the poor and sick. Theodosius' conscience was smitten, and he immediately returned everything. Without question, she was a pious woman, who evidenced an unpretentious love for the Saviour. As John suspected and later found true, she had a servant's heart. She discreetly used vast amounts of her wealth to care for the sick and poor of the city and aid the Lord's needy servants near and far. After learning about one undiscerning gift, John reproved her for indiscriminately giving away her money. He instantly liked her and developed a relationship that would endure the rest of his life. Some of his last letters were to her.

As previously noted, John seldom entertained with extravagant feasts. Almost always, he took his meals alone and ate frugally. Olympias served him his meals, and with a thin wall between the convent and the bishop's residence, she was the only one to have open-hearted, private contact with John. Some thought this gave an appearance of evil, and scandalous gossip began to spread regarding the two. While it is certain their relationship was strictly platonic, it is also certain that their feelings for each other ran very deeply.

Also, John, still keenly affected by monasticism, had a withdrawn temperament. He was not an adept socializer, especially in a world-class city that was accustomed to political glad-handing. His God, his calling and his books were his great pleasures. The more acquainted he became with the officials of the imperial court, the less he had to do with them socially. He preferred communion with God to personal interaction with courtiers, many of whom he considered to be pathetic men-pleasers. Because he distanced himself from court officials and refused personally to interact with powerful individuals, except as church and court protocol required, much disdain increased from those who could have benefited him later. He did not know how to balance himself socially.

An additional fault that caused trouble was John's sometimes harsh preaching. He was almost always warm and engaging in his delivery, especially during his panegyric sermons (eulogistic orations of formal and elaborate praise) on various martyrs. His motive in preaching was always redemptive. Frequently, he would state that he did not intend to harm his audience, but to do them good; not to kill, but to raise the dead. However, he had a temper, and occasionally this temper would overflow its banks in his sermons. Grief over the careless excesses of the rich could quickly turn into a diatribe. Weak and effeminate courtiers could not handle the normal powerful expositions of the bishop, much less his spiritually strong attacks upon their sins. They wanted easy preaching and someone who would make them feel *good*. Does that not sound like our day?

Worship

Apart from the hand and blessing of God upon him, John had another asset in his favour — the true people of God, who genuinely loved Christ, the Word, the worship and the preaching. He proved to be an immensely popular preacher, and the common believers were his greatest supporters. They thrived under the preached Word and became more Christ-like and holy. John successfully brought a refreshing degree of spirituality to the church and the saints rejoiced. He attracted and trained presbyters who faithfully shepherded their flocks with the Word. A delightful change took place in the atmosphere of worship. John's fervent and passionate devotion to the triune God, especially as he is revealed in the face of Christ, spilled over into the congregations.

Students who read John's works are given insight into the worship of the churches under the bishop's charge. He was a liturgist (one who arranges and writes orders of worship services) and the liturgy used almost every week in Eastern Orthodox churches today is ascribed to him. John possessed a keen sense of the unity in the worship between the congregation on earth and the unceasing adoration in heaven. When the minister invokes the triune God at the start of worship, 'the Holy Spirit and angels attend him, and the whole sanctuary is thronged with heavenly power'. Simply put, John viewed worship as 'heaven on earth'. In many segments of Christendom, he is known as St John Chrysostom the Liturgist.

Following the custom of his time, no musical instruments were used in church worship. There was only the rich harmony of the congregation singing *a cappella*. Centuries would pass before instrumentation found its way into the church and reached the quality so often heard in churches today. Though there are traces of hymns in the New Testament (e.g., Philippians 2:6-11; 1 Timothy 3:16; Revelation 4:11; 5:9-10), which the early churches undoubtedly employed, hymnody was still in its infancy. John incorporated these scriptural hymns into his worship services. However, Psalms were primarily sung and John made sure that whether Psalms or hymns were sung, they were sung with gusto. He believed that the redeemed nature delighted in singing God's praises and the benefits were 'support and sanctification'. Each verse may 'impart wisdom, correct our doctrines, and afford us great aid in life'. He even went so far as to say that if sung with understanding, singing 'calls down' upon the church 'the grace of the Holy Spirit' and transports the soul into the noble company of cherubim and seraphim 'near the very throne of glory.' When singing God's praises (he believed that the congregation was the choir), he exhorted the people to 'stand erect' and not to carelessly mumble the words while the 'heart is roaming elsewhere.' Citing Ephesians 5:18-19 and Colossians 3:16, John declared that singing and making melody in the heart to the Lord are clear evidences of being filled with the Holy Spirit. 'Do you wish to be cheerful?' Sing! If Christ's people sang more often, they would be cast down less.

Forsaking the assembly

John faced a problem in Constantinople that was not unlike our own (or those in between): unfaithful church attendees. Again, Christmas and Easter, along with the holy days, usually found the churches full. As usual, after the sacred seasons pass, attendance dropped considerably. To his amazement, the worst offenders were those who possessed the greatest amount of this world's riches — the affluent, the upper middle, and upper classes. The middle class and the poor, who had less of this world's goods, were usually the most faithful in attending worship. The problem was so grieving to John that he preached a homily (with the imperial family, court and praetorian guard all in attendance) entitled *To Those Who Had Not Attended the Assembly*. The addressing of this issue is found in clippets scattered throughout his sermons, but here it is in concentrated form.

He was grieved that a number found it so difficult to faithfully attend the house of God and so easy to attend a sporting event or to take care of personal and business affairs or to engage in family festivals, 'forsaking the assembly people wander away, depraving themselves by going to meetings which are thoroughly unwholesome'. No apology was made for being 'burdensome and vexatious'. He acknowledged that those who were guilty called him 'insolent and impudent'. Yet, he assured his hearers that he cared for the neglecters' eternal souls and would not cease 'annoying' those who found something else more important than the worship of the triune God on the appointed day. He was compelled for their salvation and 'virtue'. Their excuses for not attending John called 'feminine: indeed, even in their case [those] who have softer bodies, and a weaker nature, such pretexts do not suffice for justification' and those who wilfully forsake, unless they are sick or truly hindered providentially, are 'destitute of the fire of the Holy Spirit'. They should blush, he insisted, but they do not.

Furthermore, John reproved those who were present for not 'putting away their sloth' and giving 'a helping hand for the salvation of your brethren'. 'To neglect our brethren', he cried, 'is no ordinary wrong, but one which brings extreme punishment, and an inescapable penalty'. They must go after the haphazard and sporadic attendees. He reminded his hearers that 'Christianity is no child's play: no matter of secondary importance'. Jews, he stated, who lived in their inferior shadow of the Sun of righteousness were stricter in their misguided observances than some professed, loose Christians who claim to have the Light of life. People do what they want to do and the heart governs one's motives and actions, which is why people either forsake or drudgingly attend the worship of God. Their hearts are not delighting in Christ.

The preacher was not insensitive to or unaware of the struggles sincere and earnest Christians sometimes face. Hence, he instructs them:

Have you worldly anxieties? Come here on that account that by the time you spend here you may win for yourself the favour of God, and so depart with a sense of security; that you may have Him for an ally, that you may become invincible to the demons because you are assisted by the heavenly hand. If you have the benefit of prayers uttered by the fathers, if you take part in common prayer, if you listen to the divine oracles [Word], if you win for yourself the aid of God, if, armed with these weapons, you then go forth, not even the devil himself will be able to henceforth look you in the face, much less wicked men who are eager to insult and malign you.

John's view of church attendance and worship was one of grandeur, greater than going to the imperial court and having an audience with the emperor. 'For we do not commit the administration of nations or cities or the command of armies to those who enter here, but another kind of government more dignified than the empire itself'. For when one leaves a church, after the worship of the triune God, 'you have conversed with the Lord, you have been in the company of Christ'. Chrysostom rightly understood that worship was a heavenly exercise, in which the Christian entered into the very presence of God himself and to forsake it was to lose something the world, no matter how exciting, could never provide. He knew from a thorough exegesis of the Scripture that God has ordained the church and her means of grace for the salvation of the unbelieving and the holiness, perseverance and well-being of the believer. Regular church attendance greatly increased during John's ministry.

Applauding the preacher?

One issue that deeply grieved John in worship was the habit the congregants had formed of applauding during the preaching, which has relevance even for our day. Over time, he realized that it was his eloquence rather than the truth of God's Word that moved the people to applaud. At first, he simply let it pass. However, the more he thought about it, the more troubled he became. As he was making a particular point in his sermon on Acts 13:42, the congregation exploded into an interrupting applause. The preacher stopped his exposition to address the issue by saying,

> Believe me, I only speak the sentiments of my heart; if I hear your applause for my words, my human feelings for the moment are gratified. Why should I speak the truth [of God's words]? But afterwards at home, when I think how, for empty renown, the benefit of the sermon for you and for me has been wholly lost, and then I groan and weep, and feel that all has been in vain. Often have I thought of forbidding loud manifestations of applause. Let us today establish a law among us, that no hearer be permitted to applaud in the midst of any person's preaching.

Before he could resume his exposition, again overtaken by his eloquence and to John's total shock, the congregation immediately broke into cheering applause. John was more than a little irate. 'What is this noise?' he sternly asked. 'I have laid down a rule against this very thing, and you do not have the forbearance to even hear me!' Firmly, he explains that the heathen philosophers speak without interrupting applause. The Apostles preached and nowhere is it found that noisy applause accompanied their words; even Christ himself preached the Sermon on the Mount without applauding interruptions. 'If you applaud, do it in the market place for the harpers or in public processions or in theatres, but do not do it in the church. The church is no theatre.' The point was effectually made: the church is not a place for entertainment, and the preacher is not an entertainer. During the preaching, Christ is speaking, and the hearers should be quiet, resist talking to others, listen carefully, and not rudely interrupt.

5

MISSIONS AND TRIUMPHS

To regions and beyond

Throughout his short, mostly tumultuous tenure in the capital, every opportunity was taken to advance the cause of Christianity beyond the walls of Constantinople and into the dark domains and regions of the empire where there was little or no spiritual light. He was able to persevere and endure his dark trials because, among other things, John was kingdom-minded and most desirous for the conversion of the heathen to Christ. Landowners in rural districts outside the city were encouraged to build churches on their properties instead of hotels, bathhouses and shopping centres. The Phoenicians, in their vile paganism, weighed heavy upon John's heart. He sent a missionary team to preach the gospel and plant churches among them. Guided by John's vision, efforts were made to evangelize the peasants of Thrace. He raised money for missionary and evangelistic endeavours in Persia. The presence of a small Christian community today in hostile, Islamic Iran is due, in part, to John's labours.

He sent a missionary delegation to evangelize and plant churches among the nomadic Goths who lived along the lower Danube. One Sunday, and without any explanation, John brought an orthodox Goth convert into the pulpit of the Holy Wisdom Church and had him read and explain a portion of Holy Scripture in his indigenous language. Their bishop wanted an example of the power of Christ and him crucified set before his sophisticated congregation. Can you imagine the surprise and offence those cultured Greeks, who took great pride in their beautiful language, must have expressed to hear the Word of God spoken in such a crude tone and harsh-sounding language? When the young Goth finished, John immediately rose and said,

> Where are the doctrines of Plato, Pythagoras, and the great men of Athens? They have perished. And the doctrines of fishermen, publicans, and tent-makers [where are they]? Not only among the Jews and Greeks, but also in the language of barbarians, as you have this day heard, they shine clear as the sun. Scythians and Thracians, Sauromatians and Moors, and those who inhabit the remotest parts of the earth, have received this doctrine into their language, and from it have learned true wisdom. Wherever you go, you will find the names of these fishermen [the Apostles] in every mouth. The power of the Crucified has opened the way for them everywhere, has made the ignorant wise, and has given to the unlearned a greater power of speech than is possessed by the masters of language.

John's interest in promoting Christianity among those whom the Greeks would have considered barbarians was, at that time, unprecedented.

The fall of Eutropius

John's ministry as bishop was not all restructuring and reform. He had three major triumphs that increased his standing in the hearts of the people and, to a degree, the court. Each victory reveals another godly aspect and insight into this principled servant of Christ. John's life story would not be complete without a retelling of these episodes.

The first triumph was the fall of the consul and chief chamberlain, Eutropius. He was a eunuch, who had been born in Assyria as a pagan, castrated in infancy, and sold into slavery. He eventually won his freedom and found it convenient to convert to Christianity. He first found favour with Theodosius I by successfully completing a consulting errand to Egypt for the emperor and, thereafter, rose in rank through the imperial infrastructure. Before Theodosius' death, Eutropius entered the service of the imperial bed chamber, which meant he did more than just turning down the covers at night. He, in essence, became an advisor to the emperor. When Arcadius ascended the imperial throne, Eutropius manipulated the marriage of the young, licentious emperor by showing him a portrait of the beautiful Eudoxia. Arcadius fell for the gorgeous woman and married her, foiling the plan of an enemy to have his own daughter wed the emperor. Then, Eutropius orchestrated the murder of that enemy, a Praetorian prefect named Rufinus, who was given the command by Theodosius himself to watch over the young ruler. With these swift political manoeuvers, the chief chamberlain quickly gained exceptional access to the emperor and strictly controlled the access of others to him. For the next four years Eutropius took over the role of the emperor's advisor, and he became virtually in control of the eastern government. This allowed almost unrestrained dominance over the undisputed head of the empire and church.

Here is a man in the highest, officially Christian, court of the empire. He was proud of his ascendancy from slavery to a courtier, ambitious to the core, and ruthless in his dealings (he brought down two prominent generals whose properties he coveted). He bought and sold offices and positions, was overtly boastful, and, for whatever reason, was the darling of the dimwitted young emperor. In early 399, Eutropius was made a consul (similar to a secretary of state or minister of foreign affairs) and a patrician. He was at the height of his power just after John came to Constantinople.

Though no one really knows what took place in the emperor's privy council, most historians believe it was the strong pressure exerted by Eutropius that swayed Arcadius to choose John as bishop. John owed his position (humanly speaking) to the patronage of this powerful politician. Eutropius liked John at first but, very soon after his installation as bishop, he clashed with him over the issue of sanctuary. Sanctuary allowed condemned persons to find refuge in a church (especially a cathedral), free from military and governmental intervention, until a legal appeal could be made to a higher authority. Before John arrived as bishop, Eutropius pushed legislation through the imperial senate that banned the doctrine and practice of sanctuary. John believed strongly in its sanctity (it was canonical) and pushed hard for legislation against it to be repealed. Eutropius opposed John's push because, previously, several of his enemies had fled to churches for sanctuary and had escaped his wrath. However, John had the support of the senate and won the repeal. Eutropius was incensed and would, from this point on, oppose John at every opportunity.

Powerful men, especially unscrupulous and arrogant ones, always have enemies. Eutropius' opponents were many throughout the ranks of the imperial court. He had trampled upon, reduced in rank and standing, impoverished and humiliated too many powerful people to remain unscathed. Numerous ones plotted his overthrow. However, Eutropius' foolish pride was his own undoing. Here is a classic example of the biblical teaching that 'Pride goes before destruction, and a haughty spirit before a fall' (Proverbs 16:18).

One day, while Eutropius was arguing with Empress Eudoxia, he allegedly boasted that he could have her removed from the palace as easily as he had had her brought in (i.e., arranged her marriage to the emperor). Offended by his insulting remark, the empress took their two little children in her arms to Arcadius and emotionally repeated the eunuch's boast. No doubt she was melodramatic. In rare form, the emperor roused himself and erupted into a violent tirade. He ordered Eutropius to come before him immediately and, without allowing any explanation or defence, summarily stripped him of all imperial positions and offices. His enemies rapidly obtained orders to have him arrested. In sheer panic and fearing for his life, the once mighty lion fled like a mouse. How ironic that he sprinted to and sought sanctuary in the *Hagia Sophia* (the bishop's cathedral), fleeing to the very one whom he had so wickedly opposed!

Suddenly, John faced a personal and moral dilemma. With the eunuch shaking like a leaf and clinging to the altar, what would the bishop do? How would John respond to this once powerful, though now fallen, enemy? Would John yield to his emotions of the moment or act on established principle? Without hesitation, he allowed Eutropius sanctuary. News quickly spread of Eutropius' fall and his clinging to the altar of the main church. Crowds of people surrounded the church and called for his expulsion from the holy place. Police units gathered in front of the palace shouting his crimes and demanding his execution. The city was in a riot. Armed government officials were dispatched to arrest this once powerful magistrate. John, who was governed by a higher authority, would not even permit the officials into the church, much less allow them to arrest Eutropius. No one was more suited to defend, on principle, the church's belief in sanctuary. The eunuch was crafty indeed. That afternoon even Emperor Arcadius, who had just a few hours before stripped Eutropius, appeared before the mob and attempted to bring some calm. He pleaded with the crowd and asked them to be merciful. After much angry yelling and murmuring, the people dispersed. This was on a Saturday.

Sunday morning came, and the church was filled with people trying to get a glimpse of Eutropius hiding behind a sheer veil and clinging to a pillar of the altar. John used this as an opportunity to preach what many believe was one of his most spellbinding sermons, from the text 'Vanity of vanities! All is vanity' (Ecclesiastes 1:2). The preacher began by speaking directly to the cringing fugitive. 'Where are now the brilliant surroundings of your consulship? Where are the gleaming torches … the garlands … the dancers … the curtains of the theatre? They are gone — all gone: a wind has blown upon the tree shattering down all its leaves…' From there he exposed the plundering and rapacious sins of Eutropius. John spared nothing. With the living illustration before the eyes of all gathered, John lambasted the vanity of flaunting wealth and possessions, drinking banquets, lewd theatrical shows, the emotional highs of sporting events (e.g., horse and chariot races), trampling upon others, destroying careers, and of surrounding oneself with fair-weather friends. None of these vanities can bring any comfort or hope in the end. The kisses of these sins will produce an incurable, deadly disease.

John then changed emphasis, exhorting each one to take this text into his or her personal life and heart, having a living example before their very eyes. The brilliance with which he spoke to the congregation is moving even when reading his words 1,600 years later. Then, to the astonishment of his hearers, John began to plead for mercy. This one who had given no mercy should be shown mercy. If the emperor is merciful, why should they display such wrath? Why, after they have partaken of the holy mysteries (i.e., the bread and cup of the Lord's Table) and prayed the commanded prayer 'Forgive us our debts as we forgive our debtors', should they be so demanding and vengeful upon their debtor? Then he finished, with the promise that if they showed mercy to Eutropius they would have the approval of God, the commendation of the emperor, and the admiration of the ends of the earth.

The people were briefly appeased. During the week, Eutropius foolishly escaped the cathedral and was immediately apprehended. The emperor promised him safety within the city walls of Constantinople and banished him to Crete. Within a year, his enemies mustered charges of treason against Eutropius and had him transferred to Chalcedon (outside the city walls of promised safety), where he was tried, found guilty and beheaded. This was probably late in 399, just over nine months after topping the ladder of success. How the mighty had fallen!

John's granting sanctuary and defending Eutropius
brought sharp criticism from powerful sectors, especially
Empress Eudoxia; but many rejoiced at the removal of such
a ruthless leader. What must be realized is that John was
not driven by personal feelings, but by principle. He knew
that Eutropius, who had liked him at first, had very quickly
become his enemy. Like his Saviour, John did not repay evil
with evil, but he loved his enemies and prayed for those
who persecuted him (Matthew 5:44). Here is seen grace and
character in his reaction to the fall of an enemy.

The defeat of Gainus

John's second triumph was in the affair concerning Gainus.
An imperial general in charge of an army of Goth mercenaries,
Gainus had been cheated by Eutropius' deceitful political
ploys. The general, who had been promoted by Theodosius,
had fought fiercely and bravely in defeating the empire's
enemies. However, no formal imperial acknowledgements
or compensations were given to him. Furthermore, he was
aware that among the influential circles of the Theodosian
court there was a dogmatic belief that the growing power of
the Germans, especially in the military, must be curtailed,
and even reversed. Secretly, Gainus had formed a Goth
army, as a reserve should he need it, probably selected
from among the Danubian Legions. So, in the year 400, he
brought his private army of 35,000 to the outside walls of
Constantinople and threatened to enter the city. Like Rome,
no troops were allowed inside the capital. The only military
force was the emperor's small praetorian guard, and it was
no match for the battle-hardened Goths. A meeting to

negotiate terms was arranged, and Gainus demanded the surrender of three of his political enemies. One of them was Eudoxia's alleged lover, Count John. Again the emperor was weak and refused to take leadership, so the three men were handed over to Gainus and held as hostages.

Seething in anger over perceived injustices and still not satisfied with the grudgingly given compensations intended to pacify, Gainus led his troops into the city where they pillaged and wreaked havoc. Now the entire city was held hostage. Gainus did not want to overthrow the emperor or the government, and, contrary to how things appeared, he respected the emperor and his right to reign. Another meeting was arranged in which the emperor and Gainus met face to face. John was required by the emperor to be in the meeting. The bishop's only concern, throughout his entire ministry, was simply the glory of God and the salvation of souls. He had no political aspirations, and he detested political intrigue, but now he was drawn into the conflict.

The general's demands were few: his own safety must be assured and there were to be no reprisals upon his army; he must be fully compensated for that of which he had been cheated; he must be made commander-in-chief of all imperial armies; and the hostages must be punished for their crimes. With the Goth army garrisoned within the city walls, the emperor was powerless to resist; therefore, he conceded to Gainus' demands. To assure that the emperor would keep his word, a solemn oath was signed by both parties. Gainus, in effect, became head of the government and was in control of the capital.

Early historians give conflicting accounts of the exact times and order of events during this crisis. Even John himself is unintentionally misleading, as scholars who have studied his sermons from the period have observed. However, all are certain that John successfully negotiated the release of the hostages. Gainus respected John as a holy man and was very much aware of his pastoral concern for the Goths. Another meeting took place between Gainus and the emperor, with John in attendance, or between Gainus and John, with the emperor in attendance, in which Gainus delivered an ultimatum that his troops be given a church(es) within the city walls where they could worship. Arians were forbidden their worship in the city nineteen years earlier by Emperor Theodosius, and the Goths were committed Arians. Since Theodosius' day, Arians were obliged to worship outside the city, unless they went to an orthodox church. Gainus believed he, a general of the highest rank, and his troops, proven warriors and deeply loyal to the empire, should have equal status, not only in the empire, but also in the capital city. They must be given churches. It seemed, at first, that the spineless emperor would yield to the Goth's demand. Incensed that heretics might possibly be allowed again to have their own places of worship within the city, John inserted himself into the negotiations. The cause of Christ and truth, not politics, moved John into action.

John told Gainus that all the churches in the city were open for the Goths to enter and worship. Gainus replied that they did not have their *own* (Arian) churches. John retorted that the Goths did not need their own churches; instead, they needed to repent and turn to the orthodox faith of Holy Scripture. Gainus stubbornly insisted on this particular demand, believing it was owed him for his many years of devoted service to the empire. John did not flinch, but reminded the general that when he crossed the Danube and joined the Roman army he had nothing but tattered garments. Now, he was commander-in-chief and was even wearing the magnificent robe of a consul. He had more than received his just compensation. Furthermore, Gainus had sworn allegiance to Theodosius the Great (and his children) and was now betraying his oath with great ingratitude. Inflamed with love for Christ and devotion to truth, John then turned, perhaps with a flourish, to the emperor and boldly reminded Arcadius that as the earthly head of the church and a sworn adherent to the orthodox faith, he could not yield to such a sacrilegious demand. It would be nobler to step down from his throne than to give infidels houses of God within the city walls.

The emperor was, for once, emboldened by John's uncompromising convictions and refused to concede to Gainus' ultimatum. The mighty general was reduced to silence in the presence of the principled man of God and withdrew his demand. Soon thereafter, the people began to rise up against the Goths and eventually caused them to abandon the city. Within a few months (early 401), Gainus was defeated and killed by the Huns. His head, a gift from the Hun leader, Uldin, was paraded on the tip of a lance through the streets of Constantinople in celebration. John's fearless stance had won the day.

Conquering heresy

John's third victory was in confronting the heresy of the Anomoeans, the most radical Arians. Anomoeans, in both Antioch and Constantinople, sat under John's preaching, but would challenge his theological teachings in the streets and marketplace. John had publicly debated them in Antioch, which caused their numbers to decrease. As a more virulent strain of this group existed in the capital, John would continue preaching against them, but he took a different approach in confounding them.

Their ejection from their churches, shortly after Theodosius I came to power, did not make them go elsewhere. They continued holding their services outside the city walls and created a nuisance whenever possible. One particularly irritating practice was to assemble in the public porticoes, just inside the city gates, on Saturday nights and on the eves of festivals, and chant their unbiblical, Arian hymns. This they did antiphonally, meaning one group in one portico would chant the song, and then another group in another portico would repeat the song, and so on, until they chanted the song around the entire city wall. When the first song was sung, another began. Sleep was disturbed and tempers flared, especially at one provocative refrain that asked: 'Where are the people who *declare* the Three to be but one single *power*?' They would do this all night until the break of day. As the sun rose, the Anomoeans would assemble on one side of the city, march through the city centre vigorously chanting their anti-Trinitarian songs, exit the other side of the city, go to their respective meeting-places, and hold their worship services.

John did not sit idly by and observe these nocturnal irritations and heretical parades. The bishop planned to meet the enemies of Christ on their own ground. He organized and carried out more elaborate processions than the Anomoeans. The orthodox paraded with silver crosses and heartily sang Nicaean hymns extolling Christ and his great salvation. God's people were strengthened and encouraged by John's affirmative actions, but, as one can well imagine, there was much competing commotion. Eventually the government intervened and banned all public Arian hymn-sings and parades, which dispirited and diminished the Arian numbers. The historian, Sozomen, reports the orthodox kept these elaborate parades going, but not during the night, until late in the fifth century. Through John's spirited efforts, many of the Arians converted to the orthodox faith.

6

TREACHERY AND EXILE

There had been earlier crises in the capital, which brought a degree of disfavour upon John. Most of them were minor, but the cumulative effect soon began to weaken John's status in the court. However, there were three accelerating events that led to his eventual and final downfall. Each is filled with betrayal and ends in sadness.

Severian the serpent

The first was his division with the competing and rival bishop, Severian of Gaballa. During the early months of 402, John made an episcopal trip (visitation) to the western provinces of Asia to settle disputes and correct abuses among churches and treacherous bishops. Before departing, John delegated his episcopal responsibilities of preaching to Severian, a bishop of a church in the small, seaport village of Gaballa, just south of Laodicea. Severian had come to the capital seeking a better fortune (in others words, he wanted a larger church). Ambitious, a good orator, skilled at social climbing and charming people, he had gained favour with several high court officials. But Severian had too long enjoyed the luxuries of the capital and, caring little for his flock, he did not wish to return to a rural setting. John was trusting by nature and this often made him a poor judge of character. Because Severian was a bishop, John felt obligated to have Severian preach and lead worship in his absence, instead of a regular presbyter. This proved to be a fatal mistake.

While John was away, for almost four months, Severian cleverly undermined John's person and position before the court and with disgruntled church leaders. His sermons were suave and crowd-pleasing. No straightforward, bold declarations and warnings, just a tickling of his hearers' ears. Sarapion, John's archdeacon, reported all of these matters to John, but being so far away, there was little he could do. Furthermore, to complicate matters, a fierce altercation occurred between the archdeacon and Severian, allegedly because Sarapion refused to rise and honour Severian. Historical reports reveal major discrepancies between the two sworn testimonies of what happened.

Upon his return, John, rather than convening a hearing to investigate what actually happened, charged Severian with insolence and ordered him to vacate the city and return to the diocese that he had so long neglected. Apparently, John was in a foul mood and directed his church ushers to send the delinquent bishop quickly on his way. It was rumoured that this was done roughly and in a manner unbecoming the dignity of a bishop. This did not sit well with Empress Eudoxia, who was enamoured with Severian and had grown to enjoy his sugar-coated sermons. Her fiery temper flared and she rebuked John and ordered him to recall Severian into the city. John had no other recourse but to comply and Severian returned, taking up residence in the bishop's palace. Stung by the empress' rebuke and the egotistical bishop's deceitfulness, John gave Severian the cold shoulder and refused to talk with him. Tension could be felt throughout the court and in the *Hagia Sophia*. John mentioned in a sermon that, in his four-month absence, a serpent came into his garden and exalted himself. Everyone knew that he was alluding to Severian and that something had to be done to resolve the issue.

The resolver was none other than the scheming Eudoxia. She called John to the palace and brought her small son into the meeting. With manipulative coy and emotion, she entreated John, as the baptizer of her child, to be reconciled with Severian. Always forgiving, always gracious, John agreed. A public meeting was arranged. Both bishops made speeches of apology; John in earnest and Severian in vague, cunning ambiguity. Seemingly, reconciliation had taken place, but Severian secretly continued his dastardly plotting and joined with other enemies to undermine and dethrone John.

The Tall Brothers

The second was the Affair of the Tall Brothers. In autumn of 401, a group of weary, Egyptian monks (or brothers as they preferred to be called) showed up in Constantinople. Originally, over three hundred had fled Egypt, but some had died on their arduous journey and others had settled in different places along the way. Only fifty made it to the capital. They were led by four men who stood out because of their height. The purpose of their presence was to plead their case to the emperor, and especially to John, of their vile mistreatment by Theophilus (Bishop of Alexandria, referred to earlier).

Initially, Theophilus embraced these brothers, even calling some of them from their desert caves to Alexandria to assist him in the work of the churches. It seems that the main ambition of Theophilus was to extend the prestige of his person and his see throughout the empire. He often utilized unscrupulous methods and used people as nothing more than fuel for the fire. His opulent living and misuse of church funds was an affront to these humble men of the mountains. Disgusted with his lust for money, they feared for their souls. It was not long before many of them drifted back into the desert communes to escape the pollutions of their greedy bishop. Then, Isidore (mentioned earlier as a possible candidate for bishop of Constantinople) fell into disfavour with Theophilus over money (1,000 gold pieces) and was excommunicated. Isidore fled to the communes of the monks where the brothers received him and granted him shelter. Infuriated that the brothers received Isidore, Theophilus trumped up false charges against them of being Origenists and excommunicated them. He also sent notifications of his charges and actions to every metropolitan area of the empire. Harassed and not permitted to partake of Holy Communion, the monks felt they had no other alternative than to appeal directly to the emperor and John.

When the Tall Brothers arrived in Constantinople, they met with John and immediately fell on their faces. Wisely, they told him their complaints. John knew the awkwardness of the situation. He had no ecclesiastical authority in this matter due to the fact that Egypt was beyond his jurisdiction and before him was a potentially volatile conundrum. He took great care to honour all rules of canonical law and did not house them in the bishop's palace, as was the usual custom, but lodged them in a nearby hospice. He then summoned the hired agents of Theophilus who lived in the city and asked them to tell him the story behind the fugitives. To John's surprise, the agents admitted that the Tall Brothers had been wickedly treated. John took two steps to rectify the tense situation. First, he forbade the monks to talk about their grievances against Theophilus; and second, he sent a warm personal letter to Alexandria's patriarch entreating him to receive back these monks and be reconciled to them.

Before John's letter arrived in Alexandria, Theophilus had already learned of the Tall Brothers' arrival in Constantinople, and he realized that he had to limit the damage. Also, he sensed that here was an opportunity to rid himself of two prickly and hated thorns: the monks, who had discovered and could expose his extravagant lifestyle, and John, who had the fame and position he so coveted. Unsanctified minds, mingled with political intrigue, can create messy situations. Such was this affair, convoluted and ungodly. To protect himself, Theophilus sent a delegation of hermits and clerics to Constantinople to act on his behalf. He enlisted an anti-Origen heresy hunter named Epiphanius to convene a synod of Cretian bishops that condemn certain teachings of Origen. Then he wrote biased letters making himself look faultless, sent another delegation of skilled operatives to the capital with fabricated materials to spread misinformation about the Tall Brothers and John, and wrote a condescending reply to John's letter. By this time, John's prestige had started to wither in certain seats of government.

All of these malicious lies had their intended effect. They damaged John in the eyes of an imperial court — a court that wanted to believe the falsehoods.

The monks from Egypt knew that John's hands were tied and decided to appeal their case directly to Arcadius. On their way to the palace, the monks providentially encountered Eudoxia travelling in her coach to visit a martyr's shrine. They poured out their complaints against Theophilus, told of his sins and abuses, asked her to investigate their claims, and pleaded with her to require the Alexandrian patriarch to come to the capital and stand trial before John. Eudoxia was moved by the humble entreaties of these unpretentious men, and, for once, she showed some grace and promised to help them. There is no doubt that the empress set the next steps in motion.

Immediately, an imperial summons was dispatched to Alexandria demanding that Theophilus appear in Constantinople with all haste and give an account of the allegations made against him. Also, the delegated representatives sent by Theophilus were arrested, taken to court, and ordered to supply proof of their libellous claims against the Tall Brothers and John. If they could not, they would have to pay the penalty required by law for slander, which in most cases would be death. The terrified detainees quickly shifted all the blame onto their superior, Theophilus, stating they were acting under his specific orders. Nevertheless, they were jailed until proofs of their slanderous charges were produced. Sentencing was postponed pending the arrival of Theophilus.

A crafty and deceptive wolf like Theophilus is not easily trapped. Of course, he had to obey the imperial summons, but he delayed his departure for as long as possible so he could plan, not a defence, but a counter-attack. When he did finally set out for the capital, he took the long land route, instead of the faster sea voyage (about three weeks). This afforded time for his vile offensive to be in place when he arrived. Along the way, he lied about John and gathered support from other bishops.

The Synod of the Oaks

The two previous tragedies set the stage for the final one, which was the diabolical convening of bishops by Theophilus with the intent of deposing John. In late August of the year 403, over a year since he had been imperially summoned to the court, Theophilus arrived in the capital. Actually, he arrived in Chalcedon, a suburb of Constantinople on the other side of the Bosporus. Here he stayed at the Oaks, the palace of an Egyptian bishop who had once been a friend to John, but was now an enemy. Theophilus began to implement his wicked plans with elaborate care. Having already been in contact with Severian, who was mentioned in the first tragedy, he summoned him to his dwelling, along with a number of other bishops John had deposed on his Asiatic visitation. Including the entourage of twenty-nine Egyptian bishops Theophilus brought with him, there were altogether thirty-six bishops, all hateful enemies of John. What these men devilishly conceived and brought about is known as the Synod of the Oaks.

Numerous historical accounts of what took place, against and for John, are available for study. These differing reports highlight the difficulty of ascertaining what actually transpired. Historians still debate the varied aspects of the entire episode. However, in spite of the conflicting and competing reports, several things are known for certain. Firstly, Theophilus and his minions manipulated the court, especially the emperor, onto his side. Theophilus was the one who was supposed to be on trial; however, through political intrigue, bribery and threats, the situation was reversed and John was placed on trial. With Arcadius and Eudoxia siding with him, Theophilus was free to enact the synod. Secondly, twenty-nine false charges were fabricated against John. Only one had even the slightest merit: John had sold some church possessions during his Asiatic visitation and pocketed the money. It is true that John had sold the possessions, but it was later proved (after the synod) that John had deposited the money in the church's charitable fund that was used to build hospitals and orphanages. But the proof had come too late. Thirdly, on four occasions John was summoned to appear before the synod and answer the charges. He stubbornly refused citing that: a) the synod was not lawfully convened, the overwhelming majority of the bishops (thirty being Egyptian) seated on the synod had no authority to adjudicate outside their own ecclesiastical jurisdictions; b) all the charges were invented by disqualified men who were driven by evil motives; and c) he was not being tried by his peers, but by those who were all his sworn enemies. Since the proceedings were contrary to established canonical law, he declined to dignify the ecclesiastical assembly with his presence.

Several friendly bishops tried to come to John's defence but were forcefully turned away or threatened with death. John's refusal to answer to the illegally-called synod further angered the spineless Arcadius. Thus, when the synod pronounced John guilty and thereby unfit to be a bishop in

the Church of Jesus Christ, the emperor readily signed the
order of John's deposition.

When news reached the city, violent demonstrations
broke out in support of John, which lasted for three days. On
the fourth evening, as John was heading for his exile on the
waters of the Bosporus, an earthquake shook Constantinople, especially the empress' apartment. Something horrible
happened; either the empress' small daughter (Flacilla) was
killed or the empress miscarried. Whichever it was, the
superstitious Eudoxia was horribly frightened and invoked
her unstable husband to recall John. He re-entered the city
in early October 403 and resumed his labours with adul-
ation from the people, but under strict limitations from
the imperial court. Nevertheless, John's enemies were
persistent and relentless, especially Theophilus. Exploiting
false charges and lies, they again persuaded the emperor
to order irrevocably John's deposing and exile. In the early
morning of 20 June 404 (only eight months after his recall),
Emperor Arcadius sent a note to John ordering him to
vacate his bishop's throne and the city. John sent a return
note of protest to the emperor stating that he had never
been convicted by canonical law, but he quietly submitted
to the order. After intensely moving farewells (recorded
by his biographer Palladios), in close proximity to *Hagia
Sophia*, the faithful minister of God's Word silently vacated
the capital that afternoon never to return alive.

Exile and death

John's exile was from 404–407. His first place of exile was
for three years in Armenia. However, because of John's

popularity and the constant stream of visitors, an imperial edict ordered John to be transferred to the eastern shores of the Black Sea (present-day Pitsunda in the Georgian republic of Abkhazia), some six hundred miles by sea from Constantinople. Being in a weakened and exhausted state, John was taken to a nearby village chapel. He put on a baptismal robe, gave away his clothes to the poor in the small village, and died a few miles from his imposed destination. Before he closed his eyes in death, his last words were 'Glory be to God for all things'.

What happened after John's departure? For the first three months after his exile, the city was shaken by a series of catastrophic events. There were a number of earthquakes and fires, some naturally caused and some deliberately set. Then a hail storm, with balls of ice as large as walnuts, pummelled the capital and its suburbs. A few days after the hail storm, on 6 October 404, Empress Eudoxia died in agony as she was giving birth to a still-born child. Both mother and child were buried together. Throughout the empire, these events were taken as signs of God's displeasure.

The emperor, terribly shaken by these events, sent a messenger to Nilus, the well-known anchorite (religious hermit) at Mount Sinai, begging him to intercede for the city. The godly monk replied to the imperial messenger,

> Go tell the emperor of yours that Nilus of Sinai says: How can you expect Constantinople to be delivered from earth- quake and from fire after the enormities there; after crime has been established by authority of law; after the thrice- blessed John, the Pillar of the Church, the Lamp of Truth, the Trumpet of Jesus Christ, has been driven from the city? How can I grant my prayers to a city smitten by the wrath of God, whose thunder is even now ready to fall upon her?

John had left Constantinople, never to return alive, but his supporters remained. Out of love for their shepherd, whom they constantly recognized as their lawful bishop, they tirelessly laboured to have his name vindicated. The people loved their bishop and were angry at the travesty of justice against him. However hard and straightforward his preaching may have been, the people knew that he was a choice man of God, and that he had faithfully given them the whole counsel of God. Riots followed as many of his followers, called 'Johnites', relentlessly pursued his recall from exile. They refused to worship in the churches that were pastored by John's opponents. Somehow, in the midst of the riots, the Great Church caught fire and spread to the imperial palace. So great were the disturbances that the emperor banished many Johnites from Constantinople. Many refugees fled to Rome, which further spread the schism throughout the empire.

Before his final exile, John wrote a letter to the three leading patriarchs of the West — Innocent of Rome, Venerius of Milan and Chromatius of Aquila — to solicit their support against the treachery of Theophilus. Innocent took up John's cause and wrote letters to him and his loyal bishops avowing his support for John and against the malicious and unjust Synod of the Oaks. The letters arrived too late; John had already been exiled. Thereafter, a series of ecclesiastical canons were implemented by Innocent, which declared the deposition of John unlawful, and communion with the churches of the East was broken. Later, a synod of sixty-three bishops convened and declared the decision at the Oaks to be null and void. Ten years would pass before John was fully vindicated and communion between the two branches of Christianity was restored.

One definitive note of triumph must be added to the closing section of his history. In January 438 (thirty-four years after his exile), John's exhumed body was returned to Constantinople. It was met by Emperor Theodosius II, son of Arcadius and Eudoxia whom John had baptized. The emperor pressed his head against John's decayed body, prayed for his parents, and asked John to forgive them for all the injustices they had done to him. John's body was then taken in triumphal procession through the city and interred at the Church of the Holy Apostles, the traditional burying place for bishops and emperors. There it remained until the capture of Constantinople by the Turks during the Fourth Crusade in 1204. The Venetians rescued John's body and carried it off to Rome as a relic, where it was buried in St Peter's basilica.

7

PREACHING AND THEOLOGY

Returning to the questions raised at the beginning of this book regarding John's exalted status, what is the answer? It was his profound, yet simple, exegetical and expository preaching. Interestingly enough, it is believed that he never preached with notes or manuscript, but always extemporaneously. His magnetic speech, coupled with his rhetorical skills and immense knowledge of the Scriptures, captured the minds, consciences and hearts of his hearers. It is easy for others to focus on his trained and skilled eloquence and forget the unction and almighty power of the Holy Spirit. John never did. He began each sermon with prayer, invoking the Spirit's help. A form of his prayer is still used today before the sermon in the liturgy of the Eastern Orthodox Church:

Almighty God, unto whom all hearts are open, all desires known, and from whom no secrets are hid; cleanse the thoughts of our hearts by the inspiration of your Holy Spirit, that we may perfectly love you, and worthily magnify your holy name, through Christ our Lord. Amen.

What makes a good preacher?

In his book *On the Priesthood*, John devotes two chapters to what is necessary for a minister of the gospel to be a good preacher. In these chapters, one is given insight of this servant's heart and what motivated him throughout his entire ministry. What makes a man called of God a good preacher? Several principles are set forth.

1. He must be a man of the Word. Even if he could perform apostolic miracles, this does not negate 'the powerful application of the Word'.

2. He must not just possess a general knowledge, but the Word of Christ must dwell in him richly. This allows him to strengthen himself, repel the multi-pronged attacks of heretics, and comfort and protect the sheep.

3. He must confine himself to the boundaries of what God has clearly revealed. He must not speculate and make a determined effort 'to learn what He does not wish us to know'.

4. There must be 'the power of speech', the ability to communicate truth to others.

5. He must give 'attention to reading the Holy Scriptures' so that the preacher, in essence, listens to God's voice every day and learns to practise what he preaches.

6. He must 'be experienced in disputations' (arguments or debates). This is necessary for the protection and pastoral care of his flock.

7. There must be the 'expenditure of great labour upon the preparation of discourses to be delivered in public'. He made no allowance for lazy preachers who did little study or preparation for their sermons.

8. He must be 'indifferent' to the praise of his hearers. One day they may praise the preacher and the next day criticize him.

9. He must not be affected by censure or complaint, either by ignorant or knowledgeable persons. Listen, learn and improve when they are correct, but do not be cast down or negatively affected. John then notes that it is no more possible for the sea to be without waves than that a preacher be without praise and complaint.

10. He must be patient and forbearing with those to whom he preaches.

11. In his labouring at his sermons, 'this alone must be his rule and determination that he may please God'. There is a greater audience present than his congregation — God himself.

12. He must not be envious of those fellow labourers who possess greater skills and success, or be censorious of those who are inferior in this regard.

13. He must keep a careful watch over his own soul as one who must give an account before God.

14. He ought to be purer than those to whom he preaches. Though the preacher has his own struggles and cares, he

should seek to be inwardly and outwardly holy 'in order that the Holy Spirit may not leave him desolate'.

John concluded his book with a solemn reminder that the warfare of the devil against the preacher is more severe than with other believers: '...in the case of the evil one, it is not possible ever to lay aside one's armour ... for one who would remain always unscathed'. It is quite evident that John sought to implement these principles throughout his entire ministry.

Tools in preaching

Thoroughly trained in rhetoric, John employed a wide range of rhetorical devices (some would call them 'tricks') in his preaching to arrest and hold the attention of his hearers. One pulpit mannerism which became distinctly his own was the habit of striking his right forefinger into his left hand before criticizing some heretical group or sinful practice. Among the many skilful tools he used were: 1) *epanaphora* — the repetition of the same word(s) at the beginning of a sentence or paragraph (e.g., 'What is this I see?'; 'Is this to be tolerated?'); 2) *anticipation* — foreseeing the expected objections of the audience (e.g., 'What evil?'; 'What then will you say?'); 3) *arsis* — an idea first stated negatively and then positively (e.g., 'not over many days, but in a brief critical moment'. 'Don't simply applaud, but wish to be corrected'); 4) *diaphoresis* — pretended doubt (e.g., 'What can I say?'); 5) *metaphora* — application to something that does not apply literally (e.g., 'the evening of one's life'; 'food for thought'); 6) *simile* — comparing two unlike things (e.g., 'fit as a fiddle'); 7) *exempla* — examples taken from history, theatre, agriculture, sports, and a wide variety of everyday life; 8) *parison* — the juxtaposition of parallel phrases to emphasize the point:

> For there, there was a serpent setting snares,
> here, Christ is instructing us in the mysteries;
> there, Eve was working her deception,
> here, the church is being crowned;
> there, Adam is being deceived;
> here, a people is being publicly acclaimed;
> there, there existed trees of different kinds,
> here, there are gifts that are diverse and spiritual.

John had little use for allegory and his preaching reflected it. As noted earlier, his preaching in Antioch was primarily expositional homilies through books of the Bible. Despite his many episcopal administrative duties and other charitable works, John quickly resumed this practice in Constantinople. Handed down to us from that time are fifteen homilies on Philippians, five on Colossians, fifty-five on Acts, eleven on 1 Thessalonians, five on 2 Thessalonians, three on Philemon, and thirty-four on Hebrews, all from Paul's epistles. It is interesting to note, convincingly to some, that Chrysostom strongly argues for Pauline authorship of Hebrews.

True to his Antiochene hermeneutic, Chrysostom deplored the Alexandrian school of allegorizing. What his homilies lacked in homiletical style was more than compensated by his exegetical precision. His messages were theologically based but drew out heavily a moral and spiritual application. He championed the literal, historical-grammatical school of interpretation that shapes evangelical, Christian preaching to this day.

This early Greek Church Father can be credited with influencing the great Geneva Reformer, John Calvin, in expository preaching. In contrast to the earlier German Reformer, Martin Luther, Calvin appreciated the School of Antioch, which rejected multi-level allegorical interpretations and instead emphasized literal interpretation. Also, Antioch allowed for little typology. Chrysostom was a part of that school and Calvin knew that 'he never strayed from a clear elaboration and explanation of the biblical text' and spoke with the common people in mind. This impressed Calvin and moulded his own methodology of preaching. In the introduction of a French translation of Chrysostom's homilies, Calvin writes:

> The outstanding merits of our author, Chrysostom, is that it was his supreme concern always not to turn aside even to the slightest degree from the genuine, simple sense of Scripture and to allow himself no liberties by twisting the plain meaning of the words.

Themes and marks

Some of his preaching themes occur over and over. The Trinity and the eternal equality of Christ with the Father and the Spirit, being of the same essence (substance), power and glory, and salvation by the grace of Christ were never far from his thoughts. The Cappadocian Fathers may have been the greatest theologians of Trinitarian Christianity, but Chrysostom was the greatest herald to the common people of this indispensable truth. The saving knowledge of the true God was not only for intellectual stimulation, but for a purer and more fervent love and devotion to him, accompanied by holy living in conformity to Christ's commands within the community of his church and in the wilderness of the world.

What are some marks that characterize his preaching? Several are randomly noted. It was plain-style and simple (without being simplistic). Though he often had highly educated people in his audience, he spoke with the common person in mind. It was direct, almost always using the second person singular 'you'. The hearer was never left guessing about whom John was speaking. He was warm and animated, never cold and lifeless. At times he used the rhetorical device of vehemence. For example:

> *That is why I'm telling you in advance and shouting loudly that if any deserts to the lawless corruption of the theatres after this exhortation and teaching, I will not receive him into these precincts, I will not administer the mysteries to him, I will not permit him to touch the holy table.*

Another characteristic is that he was always theological. He did not shun theology in the pulpit thinking that doctrine was cold and produced coldness. Because he realized, unlike many moderns, that sound theology produces sound practice, John energetically expounded doctrinal truths in such a manner that the uneducated could understand. Passionate zeal for orthodox theology would describe the golden-mouthed preacher for ever. He was bold, not afraid of saying exactly what God said in the text. Commenting on Titus 1:3 ('and at the proper time manifested in his word through the preaching'), John declares:

> Through preaching, that is, openly and with all boldness,
> for that is the meaning of 'preaching'... If therefore, it is
> necessary to preach, it is necessary to do it with boldness
> of speech.

Joined with boldness was exhortation: 'One year has elapsed since I came to your city, and I have not ceased frequently and unremittingly to exhort you on these matters.'

Invective, which was an important form of speech for an orator intended to vilify or defame a belief system and, in some cases persons or groups, often characterized John's preaching. For instance:

> Come now, let us again gird ourselves against the unbelieving
> and infidel Anomoeans. If they are vexed because I call them
> infidels, let them flee the fact, and I will hide the name; let
> them lay aside their heretical ideas, and I will put aside this
> title of reproach.

Homiletics professors today often instruct their young students to avoid this form of speech. John knew that invective was needed to keep the sheep from following false shepherds. A cousin to invective is warning. John warned unbelievers of the consequences of rejecting Christ. He warned believers of the effects of playing with sin. He warned everyone that there was a Day, above all days, when each person would stand before God and give an account of his deeds.

The last characteristic of John's preaching was doxological. His heart would become so warm in his preaching that he would, at times, break out in praise and adoration to the triune God. Laud, honour and glory belong to God most high and John saw to it that glory was given to him, not just in the singing and prayers, but in the preaching of the Word.

Chrysostom was not a diplomat, a statesman, a philosopher, a scholar, or in the truest sense of the word, a theologian. He was, at heart, simply a preacher whose soul was filled with Scripture that burned with holy and loving fervour to the triune God. He almost always ended each sermon with these words (only with the slightest, occasional variation): 'To which may we attain by the grace and lovingkindness of our Lord Jesus Christ, with whom to the Father together with the Holy Spirit be glory, power, honour, now and ever and world without end. Amen.' Carefully notice Chrysostom's emphasis, whether they are praises or ethical imperatives; all are attainable only through the grace and lovingkindness of the triune God.

Doctrine and theology

Chrysostom lived and ministered in the young child stage of Christianity. If Christianity can be compared with the birth of a child and its growth and development into adulthood, Chrysostom's day was that of a three to four-year-old child. Remember, he was born in 349 and died in 407. He did not possess the full canon of Scripture, which was finally settled and passed into general church law at the Council of Hippo Regis in 397. There is no record he had in his Bible the books of 2 Peter, 2 and 3 John, Jude and Revelation. Major controversies and heresies such as Pelaganism,

Nestorianism, Eutychianism, and Monophysitism were
to come on the scene only after his death. Though some
scholars claim Origen developed a systematic theology,
no substantial body of divinity had been developed by
Chrysostom's time. All that had formally been adopted by the
Church were the two creeds or definitions of Nicaea (325)
and Constantinople (381). He did not have the advantage
of twentieth-first-century Christians in possessing the great,
finely-honed, creeds and confessions of the church.

The theology of this early Church Father is gathered
primarily from his expositions of Holy Scripture, most of
which were turned into commentaries. As stated earlier,
John was a preacher more than a theologian; therefore, some
of his rhetorical exuberances have been misinterpreted.
Apart from the glory of the triune God, his chief concerns
were the salvation of pagans and pseudo-Christians, and
the holiness of his hearers. When he ventured into the
theological realms, it was usually to defend the doctrines of
the Trinity and the full deity and humanity of Christ against
heretical opponents. Living in the days of a fashionable
Christianity, his preaching often stressed great moral and
ethical standards, which distinguished true Christians
from false professors. Searching will be in vain to find
clearly defined statements of absolute predestination,
election (though he often referred to believers as the
elect), total depravity, perseverance of the saints, and
even forensic justification. Though he believed that God is
absolutely almighty (that God, not demons or man ruled
and controlled the world), that man is a desperate sinner
needing powerful, life-changing grace, that one could come
and be made right with God only through faith, and that
true believers would endure to the end, Chrysostom did not

express them as clearly as they are articulated today. What was his doctrine and theology?

God incomprehensible

Then, as in our day, people had great thoughts about mankind and small thoughts about God. There were those who thought they could know all there was to know about God. John would earnestly contend against that false, self-deluded notion.

Preserved from a massive body of his writings and sermons are twelve homilies by John, *On the Incomprehensible Nature of God.* Ten were preached in Antioch and two in Constantinople. They give us enriching insight into the God of the Bible and John's beliefs about him: glorious and full of awe, powerful and soul-stirring. These sermons reveal the quality of training he received in Libanius' school of rhetoric, a masterful grasp of Scripture, the passion he had for preaching, the insight into man's spiritually dead heart, and the key to his heavenly success. Who was John's God?

Though he dealt often and strongly with ethical and moral issues, John was thoroughly God-centred. Never was a sermon given, but what, to one degree or another, the glory, power and grace of God triune was extolled as the only remedy for all the ills of Adam's sons and daughters. This is never seen more clearly than in three homilies entitled *That Demons do not Govern the World.* During John's time there were many who seemed to excuse their resistance against evil by maintaining that the world was entirely under the dominion of devils. For John, this belief was audacious and the honour of God was at stake, and he vehemently confronted that false notion.

In the first homily, John begins with an elaborate discussion of God's prerogative to give, take away, and give again: 'he is at liberty to do all things as he wills'. The Old Testament prophetic declarations: 'Does disaster come to a city, unless the LORD has done it?' (Amos 3:6); 'I am the LORD ... I form light and create darkness, I make well-being and create calamity, I am the LORD, who does all these things' (Isaiah 45:5-7); and 'The LORD gave, and the LORD has taken away; blessed be the name of the LORD' (Job 1:21) are the opening examples to prove John's thesis. He then quotes the proponent's proposition: 'But nevertheless some dare to say that demons administer our affairs. What can I do?' This erroneous worldview continues to this day (e.g., in the 1960s, an American television comedian named Flip Wilson popularized this age-old concept by constantly quipping 'The devil made me do it').

John quickly countered this argument by immediately turning to the New Testament and expounding Christ's almighty power over a legion of demons in the deliverance of the men of Gadara (Matthew 8:28-34). All things are under divine control and do not depart 'from the order which God who made them ordained from the beginning'. Others further argue, John noted, that one person is highly exalted and another is kept in a low condition; one commits a crime and escapes while another commits the same and is caught. Is this not the work and control of demons? He offsets all their arguments by firmly asserting that these very things are 'a great work of God's providence'. Concluding his sermon, John pleads with his hearers to change their thinking and perceive God's providence. In matters 'incomprehensible let us yield to the unsearchableness of His wisdom ... For His judgments are unsearchable and His ways past finding out' (*cf.* Romans 11:33).

In John's second sermon on God's control over all things, he stressed that people are harmed, not by the devil, but by their own laziness and disobedience. Even good things can become harmful if people misuse them. Blessings come through the gospel and, if rejected, condemnation follows. He exhorted the people onto perseverance in faith and lists five ways of repentance that will keep people from hurting themselves, namely: condemning their own personal sins; forgiving the sins of others; fervent and diligent prayer; generous almsgiving; and humility.

In his final homily on this subject, John addressed the relevant questions of why God permits good and evil, along with the devil, to coexist in the world. The devil cannot compel anyone to transgress. All evil and sin spring from the fall of Adam and Eve, which is passed on to all human souls. Job's fortitude is used to illustrate how one refused to give any glory to the devil and, in faith, gave all glory to God for the evil that befell him. John concludes by passionately emphasizing that Christians can resist temptations easier than Job's and exhorts them to do so.

John argued strongly that even though God is in sovereign control, it is man's full and undeniable responsibility, under God, to strive energetically using every ransomed power to resist Satan and all his minions and not yield to their temptations. Demons do not rule the world and Christians must stubbornly refuse to attribute to them any authority or praise. God alone is God, and he does not share his dominion with the devil.

Herein lay the secret to John's endurance, even in his last dark years and months. His body was weakened and fatigued, but he continued. His enemies attacked, but he held the field. His supporters turned against him, but he remained steadfast. His fellow bishops lied about him, but he never wavered from his Scripture-bound conscience. His friends wanted to retaliate, but he forbade them, and instead, directed them to trust in God the Lord who had ordered all things. John's life demonstrates the ancient truth written by the Hebrew prophet, 'but the people who know their God shall stand firm...' (Daniel 11:32). John's God is eternal, infinite, just, holy, almighty, ever-present, all-knowing, wrathful, ever-loving, ever-gracious, ever-wise. We can know him and comprehend him, but only in part. He is near us, even as close as our breath, but we cannot know and comprehend him as he knows and comprehends himself. That is why his saints shall spend all eternity learning and comprehending the God who is incomprehensible.

Christ magnificent

Being a staunch Nicene Christian, John thought much and made much of Christ. It was not unusual for him during a sermon to burst into adoration and exaltation of the Saviour, even in sermons of unusual topics. Listen as he preaches the sermon entitled *On the Fall of Eutropius*:

> Wherefore was He called the way? That you might understand that by Him we have access to the Father. Wherefore was He called the Rock? That you might understand the secure and unshaken character of the faith. Wherefore was He

called the Foundation? That you might understand that He upholds all things. Wherefore was He called the Root? That you might understand that in Him we have our power of growth. Wherefore was He called the Shepherd? Because He feeds us. Wherefore was He called a sheep [lamb]? Because He was sacrificed for us and became a propitiatory offering. Wherefore was He called the Life? Because He raised us up when we were [spiritually] dead. Wherefore was He called the Light? Because He delivered us from darkness. Wherefore was He called an Arm? Because He is of one substance with the Father. Why was He called the Word? Because He was begotten of the Father. For as my word is the offspring of my spirit, even so was the Son begotten of the Father. Wherefore is He called our Raiment? Because I was clothed with Him when I was baptized. Why is He called a Table? Because I feed upon Him when I partake of the mysteries [bread and wine]. Why is He called a House? Because I dwell in Him.

This magnificent Christ was never far from John's thinking or preaching.

Life-changing salvation

Expounding the Gospel of John, Chrysostom declared the necessity of divine grace as the cause of every good action, noting that humans can do no good thing at all, except they are aided from above (John 15:5). However, he believed that a profession of Christianity which was not evidenced by a change of life (contrary to the fashionable trends of his day) was empty and void of grace. Preaching from 2 Corinthians 5:17, he reminded the Christians that being 'a new creation in Christ' is a work that 'has been actually done for them'. Yet, in expounding further on 'old things have passed away', he asked: 'What old things? He [Paul] means either sins and impieties, or else all the Judaical observances. Yea rather, he means both one *and* the other. Behold, all things are new'.

Several decades later, some of Chrysostom's detractors would use his unrelenting emphasis and continual stress on human responsibility and personal holiness to argue that he held to an unbound, unfettered free will and was actually a Pelagian. It was the great Doctor of Grace, Augustine the Bishop of Hippo, who came to John's defence on this fallacious accusation, citing specific sections of John's works to demonstrate John believed that salvation was by grace alone. Augustine further argued that, rather than being a Pelagian, Chrysostom was a truly balanced and thorough expositor of God's free and almighty grace. Philip Schaff, the famous nineteenth-century church historian, concludes Chrysostom's views of sin, grace and salvation by stating: 'Thus Augustinians and Semi-Pelagians, Calvinists and Arminians, widely as they differ in theory about human freedom and divine sovereignty, meet in the common feeling of personal responsibility and absolute dependence on God. With one voice they disclaim all merit of their own and give glory to him who is the giver of every good and perfect gift and works in us "both to will and to work, for his good pleasure" (Phil. ii. 12)'. Such was John Chrysostom.

Christ's Church

Concerning ecclesiastical matters, Chrysostom's day had overthrown the apostolic simplicity of pastors and deacons

(Philippians 1:1; 1 Timothy 3:1-13). A more advanced hierarchical or episcopal system of bishops, presbyters (priests) and deacons had gained the ascendancy, though in his day, bishops had no jurisdiction outside their own cities or small parochial regions. Chrysostom embraced this system simply because that was all he knew or had. He did believe in the primacy of the Bishop of Rome, as the successor to the apostle Peter, but as Schaff notes: 'He conceded to the pope merely a primacy of honor, not a supremacy of jurisdiction' and there is no 'language of submission to an infallible authority'. No trace of confession of sin to a priest as a church ordinance, no absolution for sin given by priests, no worship of Mary, no slightest hint of purgatory can be found in any of his works.

Though he believed strongly in conversion before baptism, as his own testimony proves, there is much inconsistency in his belief that baptism regenerates. It is this author's assessment, though others strongly disagree, that John's inconsistency is simply his understanding that baptism *seals* saving grace rather than *confers* saving grace. In regeneration, a believer is put *in* Christ and at baptism the believer puts *on* Christ (Romans 13:14). He had high views of the Lord's Supper, believing there was a real presence of Christ in the bread and wine, but 'it would be unjust to press his devotional and rhetorical language into the service of transubstantiation, or consubstantiation, or the Roman view of the mass'.

Throughout his sermons, one will find Chrysostom directing the believer to confess his sins directly to God alone. He did not believe the human minister bestows grace; only the Holy Spirit could do such work. The belief that Mary was the 'mother of God' did not emerge until decades after his death. When he did speak of Mary, as in his homilies on the Gospel of John, she is not exalted or almost divine. There will be a resurrection from the dead and all will be judged at the Last Day. People will either go to heaven or hell for all eternity, there is no limbo or purgatory in between. In these aspects, Chrysostom is orthodox and evangelical.

8

LESSONS TO LEARN

Chrysostom's life and ministry are filled with many lessons that can be easily learned by both the minister and layperson, if there is the exertion of the slightest effort. It is the author's firm conviction that, just as the Old Testament events and examples were written for the Christian's admonition and learning (Romans 15:4; 1 Corinthians 10:6, 11), even so historical, Christian biography can be instructive. What lessons, then, can be learned from the life and times of this man of God, mighty in the Word?

Firstly, it is dangerous and can be destructive when the State controls or tries to control the Church of Jesus Christ. Once Constantine became emperor and established Christianity as the state religion, the Church was wrongfully placed under the control of the State. The Word of God no longer dictated what was to be believed, what actions should be taken, and who was to lead. Emperors and, later, kings often enacted unjust laws and installed ungodly men into high positions of leadership and banished or exiled holy men from such offices. Christ's rightful authority, as Head of the Church, was usurped by political expediency. God determined that Christ should rule in his churches and they should be under the sole and perfect authority of the Holy Scriptures, not the whims of imperfect potentates or government agendas. Whenever the State controls the Church, confusion, heresy and all forms of ungodliness creep in among the people of God.

Secondly, fashionable and popular Christianity is a blight on the genuine progress of the gospel. The gospel is divinely revealed from heaven (1 Corinthians 15:3-4) and is radically and diametrically opposed to the philosophies and mindset of this world system. The message of Jesus Christ still retains its ancient power and there are times when this power exhibits itself in life-changing and history-altering situations. This is wonderful, but it can become a curse. Fallen minds are always curious about the supernatural. Simon Magus (Acts 8:9-24) is an early illustration of how unbelievers are curiously attracted to the church and enter it without being radically changed. John faced it in his day, and we face it in our own times. People follow ever-changing popular fads and dynamic personalities, one after the other. When the fad changes or the personality passes off the scene, the professed church is left with an unregenerate nominalism void of grace, spiritual power and joyful obedience to Christ. The Spirit of God is quenched and the gospel is hindered from going to the ends of the earth.

Thirdly, it is not only good but necessary to have a thoroughly trained gospel ministry. Ignorance is not to be esteemed in the church. A good education does not constitute a call of God, but it does enable one who is called to be a better and sharper threshing instrument in the hand of the Lord. One of the reasons Chrysostom was so useful in the work of Christ, apart from the supernatural grace imparted to him at his call, was his thorough training. He had received what would be called today a good undergraduate education under Libanius. Then, after his conversion, he studied and received a rich theological education under Diodore. Furthermore, not being contented with these, he set out to memorize the entire Bible. Also, we know that he valued his books, which tells us that he continued to read and study lest he become stagnant in his own personal life and ministry. More than ever, especially in this post-modern day, a thoroughly trained gospel ministry is needed.

The fourth lesson is that menial service to Christ in his church prepares us for greater usefulness. In this day of superstars and rock stars, everyone wants to start out on top. Few are willing to do the small, unheralded tasks in Christ's churches and kingdom that are so necessary to smooth functioning and gospel success. Young men graduating from seminary are eager and willing to assume the pastorate of a large, established church, but many are quite unwilling to take a small, struggling church in a rural setting or go as a missionary to a remote region of the world where the gospel has never been proclaimed. For at least three years before ordination as a deacon, John busied himself doing those little tasks and obscure services that somebody needed to do, but nobody wanted to do. It was in these menial and unnoticed jobs that John learned humility, obedience, patience and faithfulness that would make him extremely useful to Christ in his latter years. If someone is not faithful in the smaller things, he will not be faithful in the greater things.

Fifthly, the value of memorizing large portions of the Word of God is inestimable, especially for ministers and Christian workers. John was not content with simply reading Scripture every day, he wanted to memorize it. It was not enough for him to be in the Word, he longed for the Word to be in him. Following what David claimed (Psalm 119:11), John endeavoured to do the same. Whether or not he achieved his goal of memorizing the entire Bible, he certainly did memorize large portions of it. One cannot read John's sermons or writings without seeing a wide range of Scripture verses, from the Old and New Testament, saturating his delivery. The pastor or Christian worker's success is not dependent on the cleverness of his ideas or the skill of his arguments, but on the power of the Word of God, which is 'sharper than any two-edged sword' (Hebrews 4:12). The more Scripture that is memorized and digested, the deeper the reservoir from which the servant of the Lord can draw. Gospel success can only come through the means of God's Word, as the Spirit of God makes it effectual. We ought to follow John's example and attempt to memorize large sections of Scripture. It is of immeasurable value.

Sixthly, God's providence often places his servants where they would not choose to be and, furthermore, keeps them there longer than they would choose to stay. If Chrysostom had been given a preference, he would have stayed in Antioch, where he had spent almost thirteen years of a happy and productive ministry. However, God had other designs for his servant who was filled and controlled by the Word of God. Certainly, or at least initially, Chrysostom was taken to Constantinople against his will. Nevertheless, he looked beyond the schemes of man and saw the sovereign hand of God and humbly submitted to it. He did not like the capital, with all its glitzy trappings, and would have preferred his hermit's cave. Yet, he readily took up the work and when the sleep-robbing trials, instigated by ungodly and unprincipled men, assaulted his soul, he did not abandon his post. One of his predecessors and tenth bishop of Constantinople, Gregory Nazianzus, detested the capital, resigned his office (381), and returned to a small parish church in Cappadocia in order to give himself to quiet study. Chrysostom remained, though his sentiments were the same as Gregory's. It was the providence of God, which so governed and comforted his soul, that kept him there.

Next, the fear of man can hinder gospel effectiveness. Moses instructed the tribal leaders of Israel not to be intimidated by the faces of people because God is Judge (Deuteronomy 1:17). Solomon wisely warned that 'The fear of man lays a snare, but whoever trusts in the LORD is safe' (Proverbs 29:25). Powerful political figures surrounded Chrysostom in the capital and as the bishop of the city many sat under his ministry. Yet he never wavered, or showed favouritism in preaching. No doubt he was tempted to soften his message or back away from dealing with difficult and controversial subjects or ignore the sins of prominent individuals, but he never yielded to the pressure that powerful people can exert. He did not fear the power of his enemies because he knew full well that the Lord was able to use their own power against them and bring them down. Thus, Chrysostom wielded an enormous influence for the gospel, especially among the common folk, because he feared God more than he feared men. As it has been said, 'He who fears God need not fear.' May every reader heed this truth.

Eighthly, confidence in God's inspired, inerrant Word gives boldness in ministry and endurance in the darkest of hours. Every servant of Christ senses and feels his own inadequacies; it is easy to second-guess ourselves. 'Could I have done it better?' and 'Should I have said it differently?' are questions ministers, elders and lay leaders often ask themselves in the midst of dark, spiritual battles, or at the conclusion of them. John, no doubt, asked himself these very questions and many others during his long struggles with Christ's enemies. What is interesting, as one reads his sermons preached in the midst of accusation and controversy, is that John never lost confidence in God's Word as God's Word. Time and again, he entered the pulpit, seemingly oblivious to the attack and false charges levelled against him, and vigorously expounded the Scriptures to his congregants. If there was any reference to what was going on around him, it was very subtle and only the most discerning would catch it. The Holy Scriptures were still God's inspired, inerrant revelation of himself and neither did adversaries nor circumstances alter that divine reality. John was called to preach the whole counsel of God and he never allowed outside detractors to hinder him. Because of his confidence in the Word, he boldly and patiently endured in his high calling to preach the Word to the very end (2 Timothy 4:1-2).

Then, spiritual wolves are not just found in the overgrown fields of the world, but in the green pastures of the church. Paul exhorted the Ephesian elders about 'wolves in sheep's clothing' that would come into the church and not 'spare the flock' (Acts 20:29). Ambition and self-seeking know no boundaries. Beginning with Judas and continuing throughout history, Christ's churches have had unsaved men in high places, such as the bishops Severian and Theophilus. With one breath they praised Chrysostom and opposed him with the next. Chrysostom knew the fickleness of the human heart and never let their praise puff him with pride, nor did he allow their criticisms to deter him from the work of Christ. He was never mean-spirited toward them, but he never allowed himself to get close to them. They were religious politicians, changeable and chameleon-like, blending with each scene. They were unprincipled men who used the church for their own advancement, whose aim was to climb the ecclesiastical or denominational ladder; men who loved the pleasures of this world over the joys of the world to come, who thought more of their own exaltation than the exaltation of the triune God, who laboured more to build their own name and kingdom than the name and kingdom of Christ. Unfortunately, they are still found in the churches of Jesus Christ, and they may even find ungodly protection from influential people in positions of authority. Mark them, guard well against their cleverly disguised motivations, and keep them out of office. May Christ's church never tolerate such 'false sons in her pale'.

Tenthly, when others are unprincipled in their actions we must never become unprincipled in our responses. As Eutropius clung to the altar of the *Hagia Sophia,* claiming sanctuary, John was reminded that the eunuch opposed sanctuary. Nevertheless, guided by principle, John refused to surrender him, even though he was a hated enemy of the public. He knew that he would anger some formidable individuals by his refusal, but he would not yield or give in to emotional circumstances. When his opponents slandered and defamed his name and manufactured false charges against him, he did not retaliate. When fickle politicians vacillated and changed positions, and friend became foe, he would not become unprincipled. Instead, he acted like a Christian and entrusted himself to his faithful Creator and God (1 Peter 4:19). John was not without his sins or faults, but he never stooped to the level of his enemies. When professing Christians act like the world, Christians must not stoop to their level and act like them.

Eleventh, the Christian life and ministry involve an unrelenting series of battles. John's ministry illustrates this well. It is true there are times of great blessing, peace and joy in our walk and labours; nonetheless, this world is still a battlefield and not heaven. Glory is waiting, but it is not now. The world still hates Christ. Satan's strategies have not changed; he still lays snares, erects strongholds, slanders the blood-washed saints, and opposes the progress of the kingdom of God's dear Son. That is why Paul commanded the Ephesian believers to put on the 'whole armour of God' (Ephesians 6:10-19). However, our greatest enemy is not without, but within (Romans 6:17). If you have exited one skirmish, brace yourself and steel your soul for another. It is just around the corner; the war is still raging! No armistice or truce will be called until the King of kings and Lord of lords 'sweeps the field' and declares 'of His foes there's none remaining, none the contest to maintain' at his glorious appearing.

Twelfth, preaching is still the chief means the triune God has ordained to make known his Word, exalt his Son, edify and strengthen the church, and save the lost. Chrysostom understood from Romans 10:14-15 that in the preaching of the Holy Scriptures, especially the gospel, Christ himself is directly speaking to those who hear. So convinced of this truth, he would dogmatically state that preaching 'is a higher thing than miracles'. People will not hear Christ speaking unless the Word is preached. It is not in concerts, drama and Christian comedy that Christ speaks, but in clear exposition of the Holy Scriptures. When God's divinely-appointed method is faithfully used, Christ will be exalted, the church will be built up and made holy, and the lost will be saved. That is why Chrysostom primarily gave himself to preaching, and that is why men called of God should 'in season and out of season' do the same.

Thirteenth, those who find Christ precious to their souls die well. That is not the case with unbelievers, unless they are heavily medicated or deceived. Years filled with ministerial hardship, church intrigue and spiritual warfare can often leave one bitter and resentful, and such things have caused some even to abandon the church. This has happened to ministers and laymen. Not so with John. If, in his letters, he explains that he is cold and tired, he is not complaining, but making a statement of fact. Rather than feeling sorry for himself during his exile, he pressed on with hope and confidence in God's sovereign providence. He wrote letters of wonderful encouragement and spiritual instruction to a host of saints. As the day of his death drew near, without any bitterness or evil-speaking against those who did him so much harm, he calmly prepared for it. How could he do so? Because his faith was firmly fixed on Christ, who was not only the author and finisher of his faith (Hebrews 12:2) but precious to his soul (1 Peter 2:7). Somewhere along the way, the false prophet Balaam watched a justified person die. Later, he would request: 'Let me die the death of the righteous, and let my end be like his!' Chrysostom exemplified what Balaam and others through the centuries have observed — that those who treasure Christ die well. Only a true Christian can say as his last words: 'Glory be to God for all things.'

Fourteenth, the Lord may bury his workers but not his work. God buried Moses in the land of Moab, beyond the

Jordan (Deuteronomy 34:1-6), but the work of the kingdom moved forward under the leadership of Joshua. John died, but the work of God did not die with him. From Stephen, the first martyr of the Christian Church, to the present day, untold servants of Christ have lain upon their beds of death to work no more. The first question that usually comes to mind at the death of a prominent servant of Christ is: 'What will happen now?' While people may wonder, God does not. He already has another servant waiting in the wings that he will raise up to carry on the great work that Christ accomplished at the cross. Jesus' own promise will not fail. He will build his church, and 'the gates of hell shall not prevail against it' (Matthew 16:18). In the grand scheme of things, the worker is insignificant, but the work is not. Many more Christian workers may go to their graves before Christ returns and, while we may lament their passing, we must spend and be spent, confident that the work of God will continue on the earth until every last purpose is fulfilled.

Finally, any belief other than a well-rounded Trinitarian Christianity is false. Since the days of Freidrich Schleiermacher and Albrecht Ritschl, along with other liberal theologians of their ilk, who taught that the doctrine of the Trinity was unimportant to Christianity and no longer needed, evangelicalism has gradually slid in that direction. Chrysostom would vehemently disagree with that heretical idea. He did not consider the Arians and Anomoeans simply misguided Christians, brethren that needed to be patiently loved or ones with whom he could worship and work. They were enemies of the 'only begotten Son of the Father' and his cross, and their soul-damning doctrines must be denounced and opposed at every turn. He stood firmly and without equivocation upon the creed of Nicaea and the definition of

Constantinople, not because the church crafted them, but because he knew and believed these doctrinal statements to be the exegetically clear and unadulterated teachings of Holy Scripture. Today, more than ever in Christianity, there is the need to return to biblical Trintarianism, without which there is no eternal life.

CONCLUSION

It is good that Christ reigns over all, particularly in his church. Otherwise, biblical Christianity would disappear from the earth. Chrysostom is proof positive that the mediatorial Lord of heaven and earth rules and overrules in the affairs of men and that he sometimes takes his servants through dark and soul-jarring providences to cause his Word to triumph at last. Chrysostom also demonstrates that men of God can faithfully (by the sustaining power and grace of Christ) expound the whole counsel of God and leave a lasting mark upon Adam's fallen race, even when wicked people and all the forces of hell converge against their souls. As long as the history of Christianity is studied, the name *Golden Mouth*, this preacher mighty in the Word, will never be forgotten.